Contemporary Chord Workbook book 1

by Margaret Brandman

Exclusive Distributors for Australia and New Zealand
Encore Music Distributors
6 Abbott St
Alphington 3078 Victoria
Australia
Ph +61 3 9415 6677
Facsimile 61 3 9415 6655
Email sales@encoremusic.com.au

This book © Copyright 2024 by Margaret Brandman trading as Jazzem Music
46 Gerrale St,
Cronulla NSW 2230 Australia
ISBN 978-0-949683-06-9
Order Number MMP8077
International Copyright Secured (APRA/AMCOS) All Rights Reserved

Unauthorised reproduction of any part of this publication by any means including
photocopying is an infringement of copyright.

INTRODUCTION

This book is intended for those students who have already gained a thorough grounding in music fundamentals. It follows on from Book Two of the Contemporary Chord Workbook series, which covers all the fundamentals of music including all types of intervals, scales and modes. In this **Contemporary Chord Workbook**, students will find a means of gaining a thorough understanding of:

- chord sounds and spellings,
- chord symbols
- the functions and positions of each chord in the various scales.
- the modes or scales which can be played together with each chord

There are plenty of exercises provided and as Treble and Bass Clef exercises are given equal weight the book is suitable for students of all instruments.

The scope of the book does not however permit the discussion of the many chord voicings available.

Piano students are advised to refer to the other linked books in the series:

1) Pictorial Patterns *for Keyboard Scales and Chords* - for a visual representation of the keyboard layout of all the scales and chords and a scale and chord practice planner

2) Books 1-4 of the *Contemporary Piano Method*, for further information on the subject of chord voicing and chord analysis techniques for all styles of music.

For information on the extended versions of the chords, (9ths,11ths, 13ths) students may continue on to Book 2 of this series.

Margaret Brandman
Ph.D. (Mus/Arts) , B.Mus.(Comp) T.Mus.A.,
F.Comp.ASMC., L.Perf.ASMC. A.Mus.A.
Hon.FNMSM., A.S.A. T.Dip

Contemporary Chord Workbook book 1

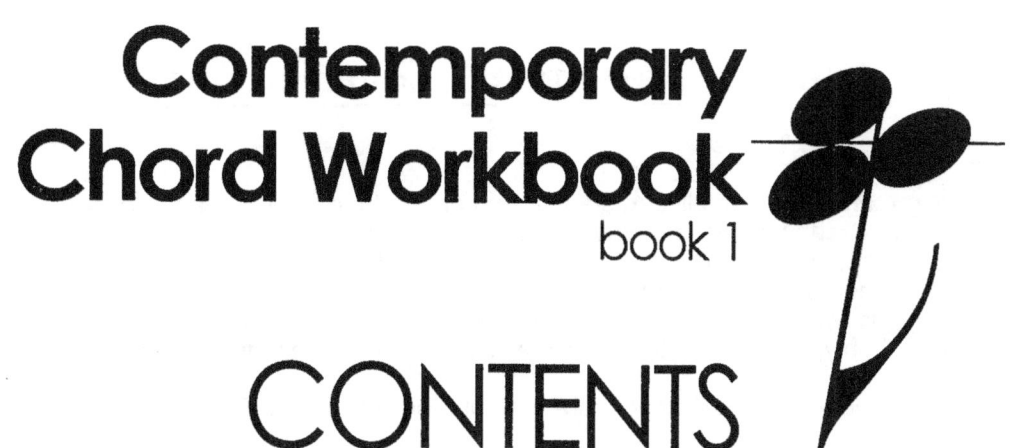

CONTENTS

SECTION 1 — Basic Elements of Chord Building.
Page
- 4 (1) Semitones and Tones. (2) Accidentals, Enharmonic Change.
- 5 Exercises on (1) and (2).
- 6 (3) Scales.
- 7 (4) The Cycle of Fifths.
- 8 (5) Intervals.
- 9 Exercises on (5)
- 10 Diminished and Augmented Intervals.
- 11 Exercises.

SECTION 2 — Triads.
- 12 The Major Triad.
- 13 Exercises. Close and Open Positions.
- 14 The Minor Triad.
- 15 Exercises.
- 16 Inversions. Inversion Figuring.
- 17 Exercises on Inversions.
- 18 The Diminished Triad.
- 19 Exercises on Diminished Triads.
- 20 The Augmented Triad.
- 21 Exercises on Augmented Triads.
- 22 The Position of the Triads in the Scales. Exercises.
- 23 Chord Tables.
- 24 Exercises on the Chord Tables.
- 25 How the Triads Function. Exercises.
- 26 The Suspended 4th Triad.
- 27 Exercises on all types of Triads.
- 28 Harmonisation of a song, "MELLOW WALTZ". Adding a Left Hand accompaniment.

SECTION 3 — Four-Note Chords.
- 29 + 30 The Modes.
- 31 + 32 Exercises on Modes.
- 33 **Seventh Chords.** The Dominant Seventh Chord.
- 34 Ways to Work out a Dominant Seventh Chord.
- 35 Exercises on Dominant Seventh Chords.
- 36 Inversions of Seventh Chords.
- 37 Exercises.
- 38 Diminished Seventh Chords.
- 39 Exercises.
- 40 Major Seventh Chords.
- 41 Exercises.
- 42 **Two-in-One Chords.** (1a) Major Sixth Chords.
- 43 Exercises.
- 44 (1b) Minor Seventh Chords.
- 45 Exercises.
- 46 **Two-in-One Chords.** (2a) Minor Sixth Chords.
- 47 Exercises.
- 48 (2b) The Minor Seventh Flattened 5th or Half-Diminished 7th Chord.
- 49 + 50 Exercises.
- 51 Chord Review Exercises.
- 52 Harmonisation of a song, "RASPBERRY RAG".
- 53 Alternate Chord Symbols.
- 54 **Two-in-One Chords.** (3) The Dominant 7th Flattened 5th Chord.
- 55 Exercises.
- 56 **Altered Chords.** (2) Dominant 7th Sharpened 5th. Exercises.
- 57 **Altered Chords.** (3) Major 7th Sharp 5. (4) Major 7th Flat 5.
- 58 Exercises.
- 59 **Altered Chords.** (5) Minor Triad with a Sharpened 7th.
- 60 The Dominant 7th Suspended 4th Chord.
- 61 Exercises.
- 62 Chord Review Exercises.
- 63 Chord Progression Exercises.
- 64 Harmonisation of a song, 'MOVIN' THE CHORDS AROUND'.

SECTION 4 — Extended Chords.
Refer to Contemporary Chord Workbook, Volume II.

BASIC ELEMENTS OF CHORD BUILDING

(1) **Semitones and Tones.**

The **Semitone** is the smallest distance from one note to the next, available on a keyboard instrument. On a fretted instrument, it is the distance from one fret to the next.

It can be written as two notes of the same name with an accidental added to one of them, or it can be written as two different note names.

The **Tone** is twice the distance of a semitone. On a keyboard instrument, leave out one key (black or white) only, and on a fretted instrument it is the distance between two frets.

N.B. For the purpose of this workbook, always write tones ONE LETTER NAME AWAY from the given note.

(2) **Accidentals.**

To write Semitones and Tones you need to know the Accidentals. They are as follows:— the SHARP (♯), the FLAT (♭), the NATURAL (♮)

the DOUBLE SHARP (𝄪), the DOUBLE FLAT (♭♭)

The SHARP (♯) raises a note by a Semitone.

The FLAT (♭) lowers a note by a Semitone.

The NATURAL (♮) cancels the effect of a Sharp or Flat, bringing the note back to its original letter name.

The DOUBLE SHARP (𝄪) raises a note by a Tone.

The DOUBLE FLAT (♭♭) lowers a note by a Tone.

Cancellation of a Double Sharp or Double Flat.

To cancel either sign, a single Natural sign is still used. However to bring the notes back to the **single** sharpened or flattened versions in the same bar (measure), both a Natural sign and a SINGLE sharp or SINGLE flat sign must be used. Thus: ♮♯ or ♮♭

For Example:

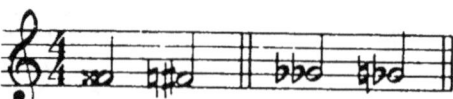

ENHARMONIC CHANGE.

This is the practice of writing the same sound in two or more different ways. For instance on a keyboard instrument F♯ and G♭ are played on the same black key (same fret for a fretted instrument) and the notes D𝄪, E and F♭ are all played on the same white key (same fret).

Accidental Chart

This chart presents the Accidentals in progressive order from **Lowest** to **Highest**, with a semitone between each one. Keep this chart in mind when raising or lowering notes by a semitone.

e.g. — The note a semitone higher than G♭♭ is G♭
— The note a semitone lower than F♯ is F♮.

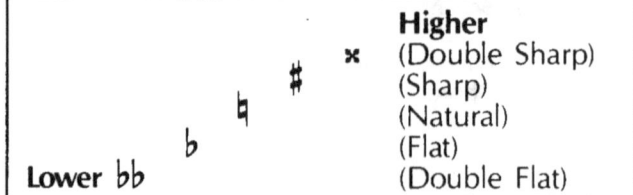

Exercise 1. Write Semitones **up** from these notes using the same letter names.

Exercise 2. Write Semitones **down** from these notes using the same letter names.

Exercise 3. Write Semitones **up** from these notes using the next letter name in the alphabet.

Exercise 4. Write Semitones **down** from these notes using the next letter name down in the alphabet.

Exercise 5. Write Tones **up** from the given notes using the next letter name in the alphabet.

Exercise 6. Write Tones **down** from the given notes using the next letter name down in the alphabet.

Exercise 7. Name these as Semitones or Tones.

BASIC ELEMENTS OF CHORD BUILDING

(3) SCALES

The four types of scale in common use in Western music (Major, Natural Minor, Harmonic Minor and Melodic Minor) all consist of a Pattern of Tones and Semitones. (T and S)

The MAJOR PATTERN is   T   T   S   T   T   T   S.

The Natural MINOR is   T   S   T   T   S   T   T.

The Harmonic MINOR is   T   S   T   T   S   T½   S.

The Melodic MINOR is   ascending   T S T T T T S   and
```
                         ^ ^ ^ ^ ^ ^ ^
                       1-2-3-4-5-6-7-8
                         v v v v v v v
```
                     descending   T S T T S T T

C MAJOR   C MAJOR

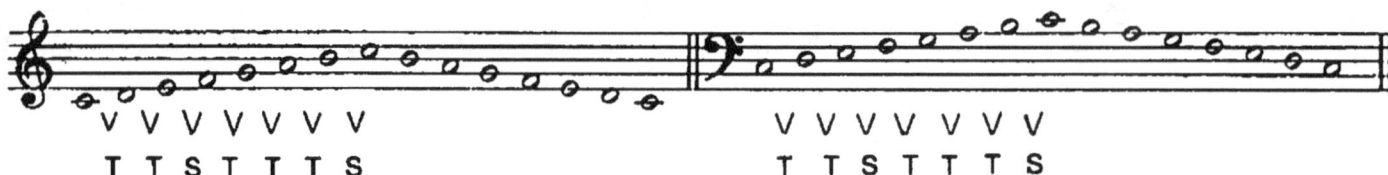

T T S T T T S   T T S T T T S

A NATURAL MINOR   A NATURAL MINOR

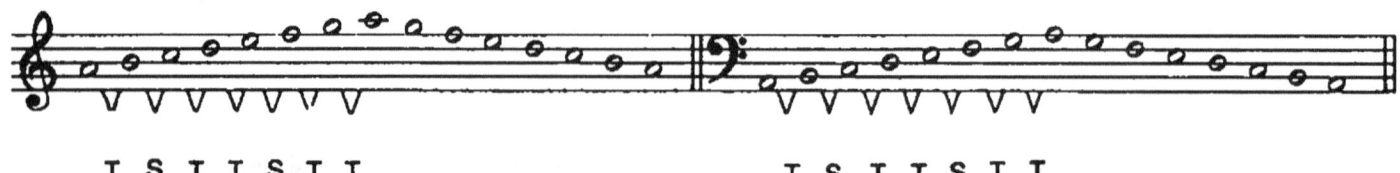

T S T T S T T   T S T T S T T

A HARMONIC MINOR   A HARMONIC MINOR

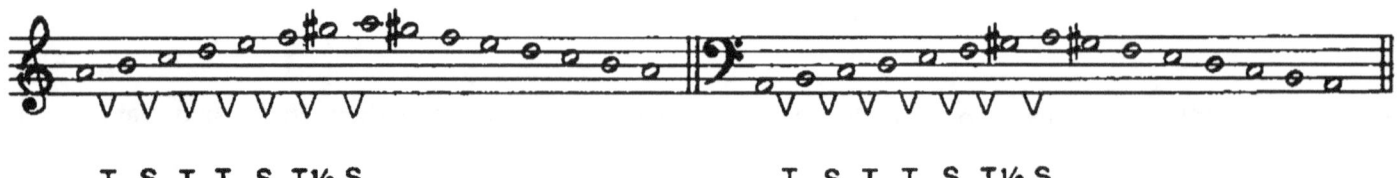

T S T T S T½ S   T S T T S T½ S

A MELODIC MINOR   A MELODIC MINOR

T S T T T T S T T S T T S T   T S T T T T S T T S T T S T

BASIC ELEMENTS OF CHORD BUILDING

(4) THE CYCLE OF FIFTHS

The Key Signatures for all the above scales can be found by studying the Cycle of Fifths. The scales with Flats are on the left-hand side and the scales with Sharps are on the right-hand side.

The reason that the Cycle is known as the Cycle of FIFTHS is that there is an interval of **Perfect Fifth** from each major note name to the next or from each minor note name to the next.

```
                    ♭        C              ♯
                         F   Ami    G
                        Dmi       Emi
                  B♭      1    0    1     D
                  Gmi  2              2  Bmi

              E♭ Cmi  3              3  F♯mi A

               A♭ Fmi  4            4  C♯mi
                                             E
                    D♭ B♭mi 5    5  G♯mi
                              6|6        B
                         E♭mi   D♯mi
                      G♭              F♯
```

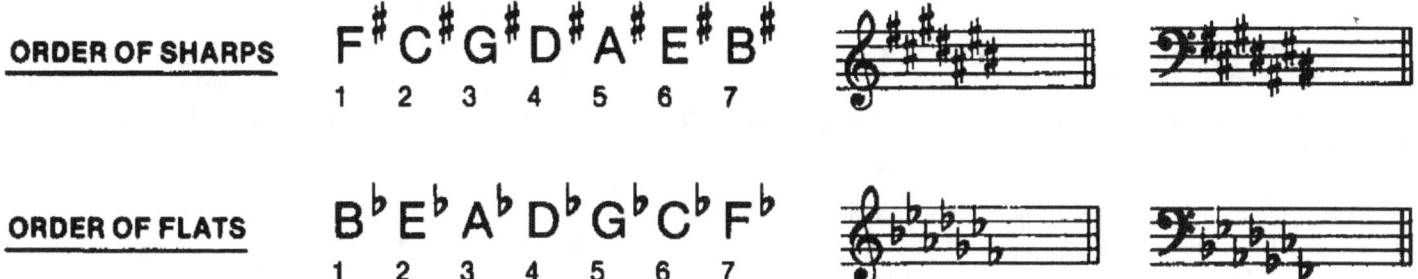

ORDER OF SHARPS F♯ C♯ G♯ D♯ A♯ E♯ B♯
                  1 2 3 4 5 6 7

ORDER OF FLATS   B♭ E♭ A♭ D♭ G♭ C♭ F♭
                  1 2 3 4 5 6 7

(5) INTERVALS

An Interval is the **distance** between two notes.

The naming of intervals is based on the intervals found in the Major Scale. For instance, the distance from C to D, (in C Major Scale) is a Major Second, from C to E is a Major Third and so on. These intervals are known as Diatonic Intervals or intervals derived from a Diatonic Scale. (A diatonic scale is a scale which uses a mixture of Tones and Semitones, unlike the Chromatic Scale which consists of Semitones only.)

The following Perfect and Major Intervals are all found in the Major Scale.

PERFECT INTERVALS — Unison, Fourth, Fifth, Octave

Four of these intervals are known as **Perfect** Intervals, that is, they are acoustically Perfect in sound — smooth with no dissonance. They are found in the Overtone series or Harmonic Series. The first overtone or Harmonic of any note is the Octave above. If you have ever blown across the lip of a soft-drink bottle and then blown harder, you will have noticed this phenomenon. On a Keyboard instrument, the unison and octave are tuned to a precise mathematical proportion, and the Perfect Fourth and Perfect Fifth are as close to Perfect as the modern tempered scale will allow.

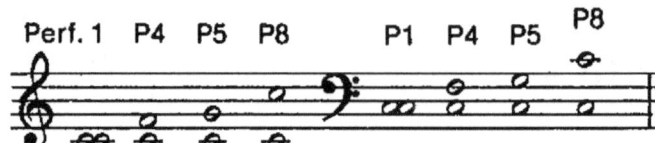

MAJOR AND MINOR INTERVALS

The other intervals in the Major Scale are all **'Major'** intervals, but the word in this case should be taken to mean 'Greater' intervals. (Major 2nd, 3rd, 6th and 7th.)

If these 'Greater' intervals are lowered by a semitone they become **'Minor'** or 'Lesser', intervals. (Minor 2nd, 3rd, 6th and 7th,). Thus 'minor' intervals are not necessarily part of the Minor scale as the terms Major and Minor mean **qualities of scale sounds** when used to describe the scales.

Therefore when referring to Intervals, always take the Major Intervals from the Major Scale and simply lower them a semitone to find the Minor Intervals.

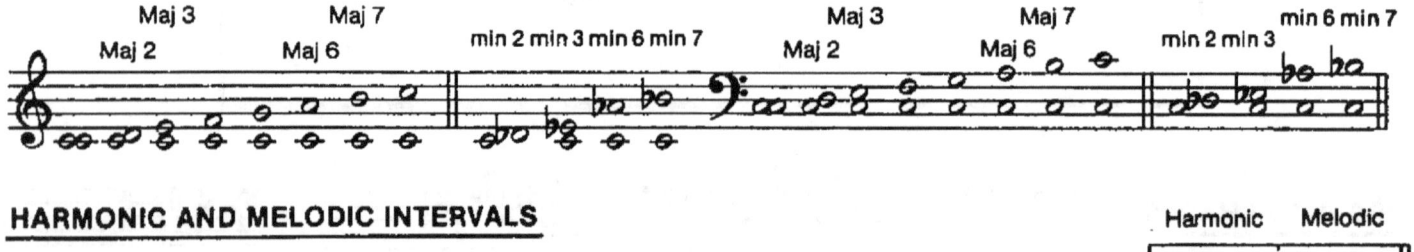

HARMONIC AND MELODIC INTERVALS

Intervals are referred to as Harmonic if played simultaneously and Melodic if played in succession.

In the following exercises make sure that the intervals of 'Unison', '3rd', '5th', and '7th' are always written from line to line, or space to space and that the intervals of a '2nd', '4th', '6th' and Octave are written from line to space or from space to line.

FOR EXAMPLE:

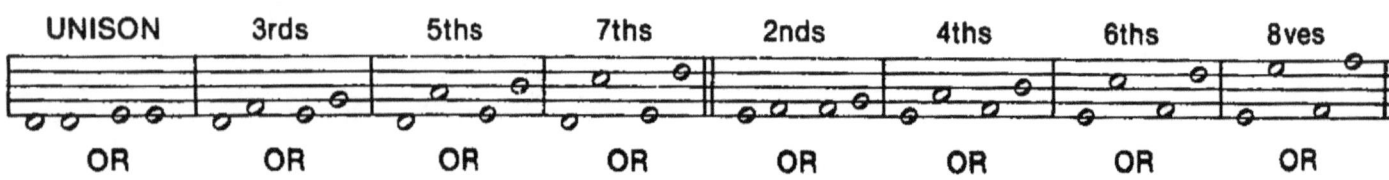

Practical Hint: To work out an interval on a Double Sharpened or Flattened Note, work it out on the closest key you are familiar with and then shift the whole unit up or down to match the accidentals.

For Example:

EXERCISES

The intervals along the following line are all taken from the G and F Major Scales. Name them.

Change these intervals from Major to Minor. T↓ or B↑
Use accidentals only, do not alter the original letter names of the given notes.
Refer to Contemporary Theory Workbook - Book 2 for the semitone formulae. ↑↓

e.g. Maj 6 min 6 Maj 2_____ Maj 7_____ Maj 3_____ Maj 7_____ Maj 6_____ Maj 3_____ Maj 2_____

Change these intervals from Minor to Major. T↑ or B↓

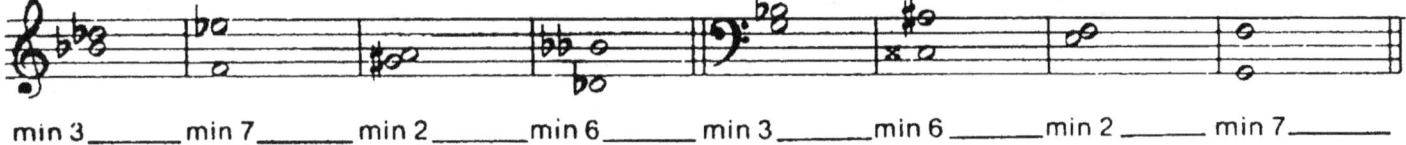

min 3_____ min 7_____ min 2_____ min 6_____ min 3_____ min 6_____ min 2_____ min 7_____

Name these intervals.

Write these intervals above the given notes.

P8   min 6   Maj 7   P5   P4   P1   min 7   Maj 2

Write these intervals below the given notes.

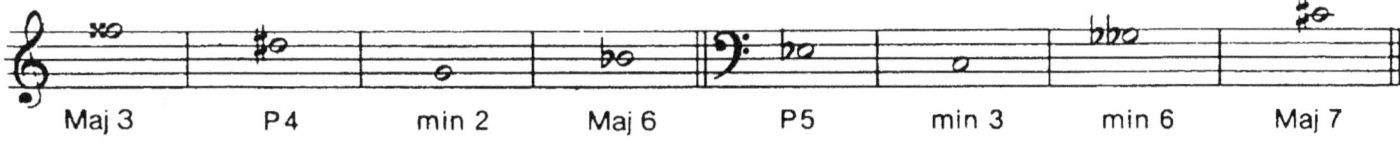

Maj 3   P4   min 2   Maj 6   P5   min 3   min 6   Maj 7

DIMINISHED AND AUGMENTED INTERVALS

When a Perfect Interval is **lowered** by a **semitone** it becomes a **'Diminished'** (smaller) Interval, for example a Diminished Fifth.

When a Perfect Interval is **raised** by a **semitone** it becomes an 'Augmented' (larger) Interval, for example an Augmented Fourth.

When a Major Interval is lowered the first time it becomes a Minor Interval and if **lowered** a **second** time it becomes Diminished.

When a Major Interval is **raised** by a **semitone**, it also becomes Augmented.

FOR EXAMPLE:

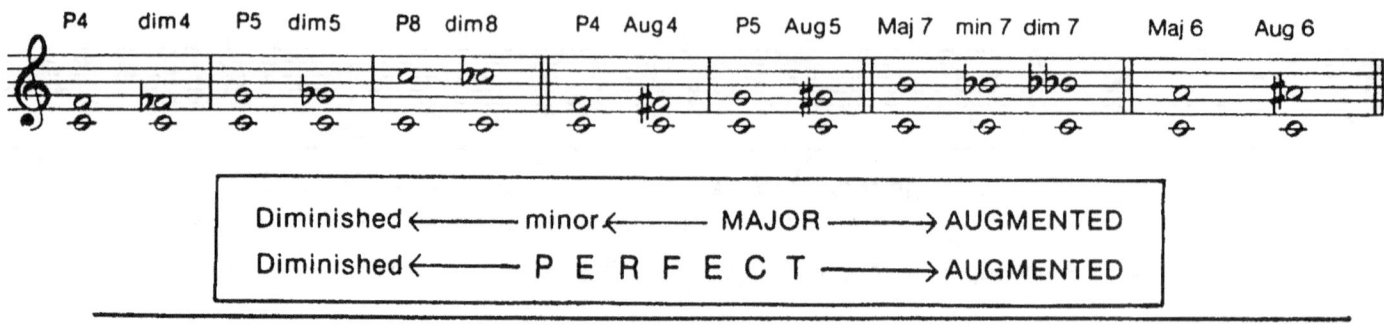

Diminished ←— minor ←— MAJOR —→ AUGMENTED
Diminished ←——— P E R F E C T ———→ AUGMENTED

EXERCISES

Change these intervals from Perfect to Augmented.   T↑ or B↓

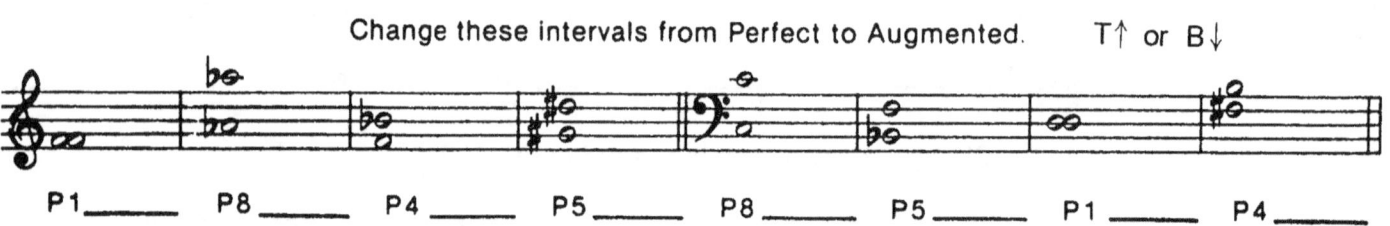

P1____ P8____ P4____ P5____ P8____ P5____ P1____ P4____

Change these intervals from Perfect to Diminished.   T↓ or B↑

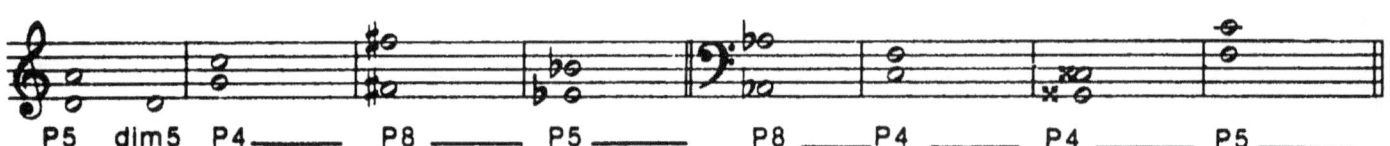

P5 dim5 P4____ P8____ P5____ P8____ P4____ P4____ P5____

Change these intervals from Major to Augmented   T↑ or B↓

Maj 3____ Maj 6____ Maj 6____ Maj 2____ Maj 7____ Maj 3____ Maj 2____ Maj 7____

Change these intervals from Major to Diminished. T↓ or B↑ or T↓/B↑ **11**

Maj 7_____ Maj 3_____ Maj 6_____ Maj 2_____ Maj 2_____ Maj 7_____ Maj 6_____ Maj 3_____

Change these intervals from Minor to Diminished. T↓ or B↑

min 7_____ min 3_____ min 2_____ min 6_____ min 3_____ min 6_____ min 7_____ min 2_____

Name the following Intervals.

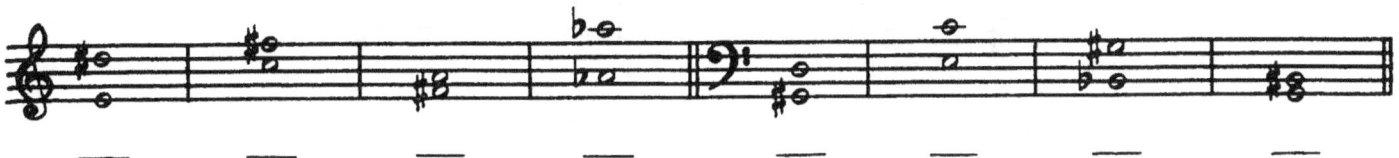

_____ _____ _____ _____ _____ _____ _____ _____

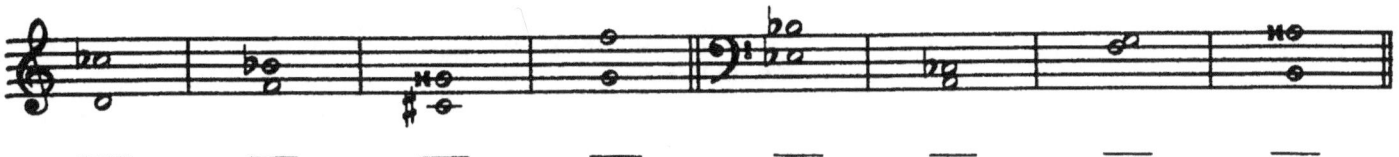

_____ _____ _____ _____ _____ _____ _____ _____

Write these intervals above the given notes.

P5   Maj 2   dim 3   min 6   Maj 7   P4   P8   Aug 2

Write these intervals below the given notes.

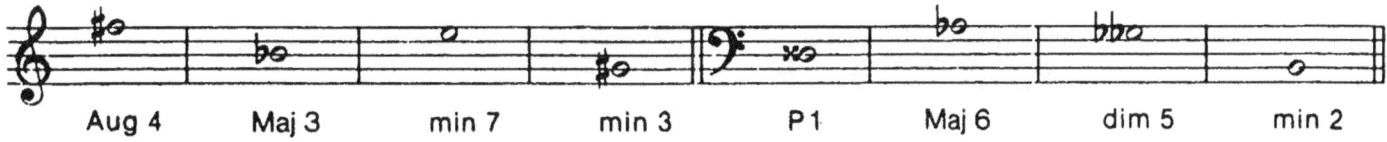

Aug 4   Maj 3   min 7   min 3   P1   Maj 6   dim 5   min 2

THE MAJOR TRIAD (3-Note Chord)

Using the building blocks discussed on the previous pages, there are 4 different ways to work out the Major Triad.

(1) From the **Major Scale**: take the 1st, 3rd and 5th notes.

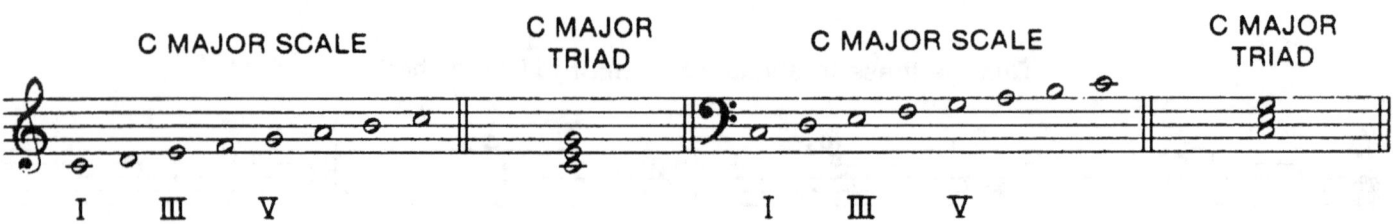

(2) Using **Semitones**: the distance between the notes are 4 semitones between the first two notes and 3 semitones between the top two notes.

(3) Using **Major and Minor Thirds**: The Major Triad consists of a Major Third between the first two notes and a Minor third between the top two notes.

        Min 3 (3 semitones)
i.e. Maj 3 (4   "   )

(4) Using **Intervals**: Build a Major Third from the Root note and add to it the interval of a Perfect 5th from the root note.

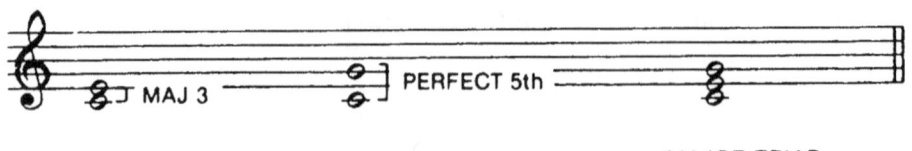
          +   = MAJOR TRIAD

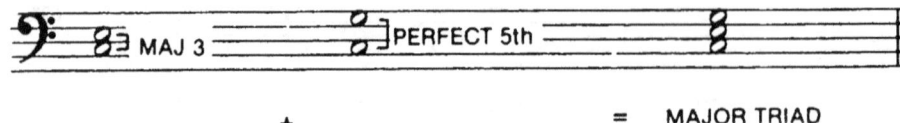
          +   = MAJOR TRIAD

A Major Chord is indicated by its letter name only. Thus: B♭

Use which ever method you find easiest, to work out the Major Chords above these Root Notes, then use one of the other methods to check your answers.

Exercise 1. Name these chords.

Exercise 2. Complete these Major Triads.

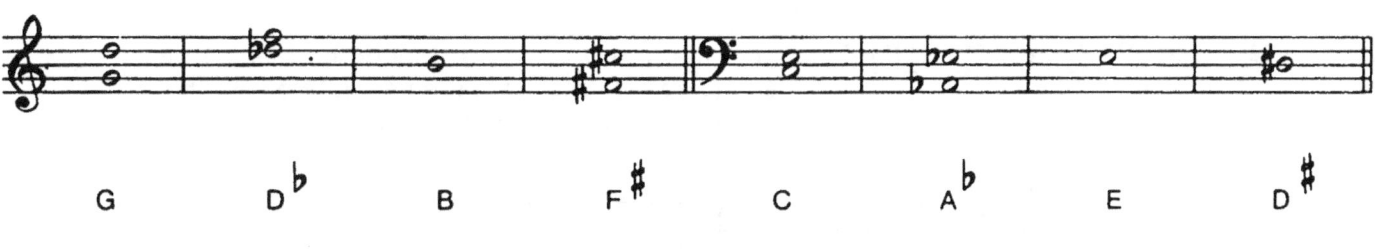

Exercise 3. Write these Major Triads.

CLOSE AND OPEN POSITION

If the three notes of the triad are placed within the limits of an octave, the chord is regarded as being in 'CLOSE' position.

If the notes are so arranged as to move over the limits of an octave, the chord is regarded as being in 'OPEN' position. As long as the Root Note is the lowest sounding note, the chord is regarded as being in Root position.

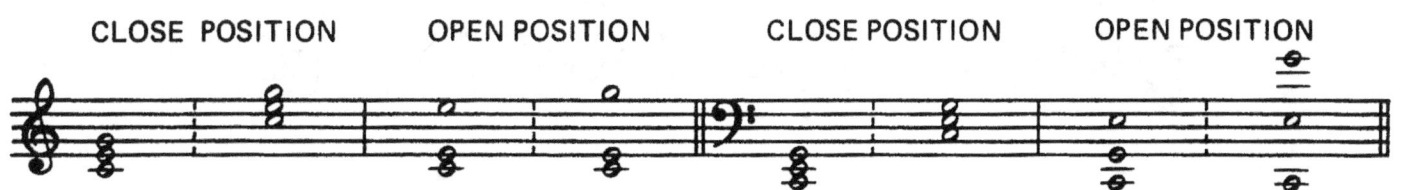

THE MINOR TRIAD (3-Note Chord)

There are 5 ways to work out the Minor Triad.

(1) From any form of the **Minor Scale**: take the 1st, 3rd and 5th notes.

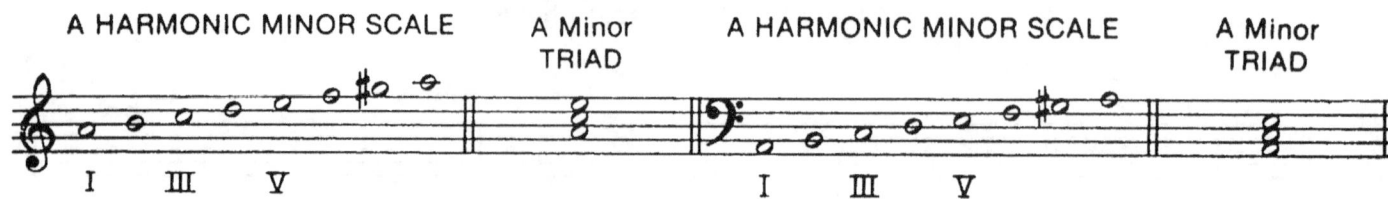

(2) Using **Semitones**: From the first note to the second note is 3 semitones; from the second note to the third note is 4 semitones.

(3) Using **Major** and **Minor thirds**: From the first note to the second note is a Minor third (3 semis) and from the second note to the third is a Major Third (4 semis).

(4) Using **Intervals**: Build a Minor Third from the Root Note and add to it the Interval of a Perfect Fifth.

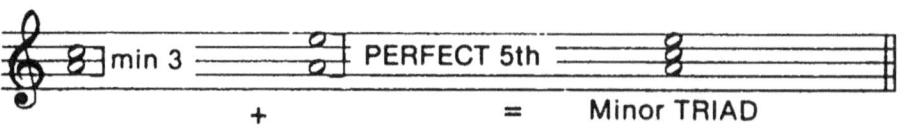

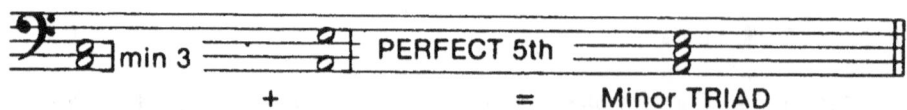

(5) From the **Major CHORD**: Lower the 3rd degree (middle note) by a semitone to find the Minor Chord.

A Minor Chord is indicated by its letter name followed by a small 'mi'. Thus: Bbmi.

Exercise 1. Name these chords.

_____ _____ _____ _____ _____ _____ _____ _____

Exercise 2. Complete these Minor Triads.

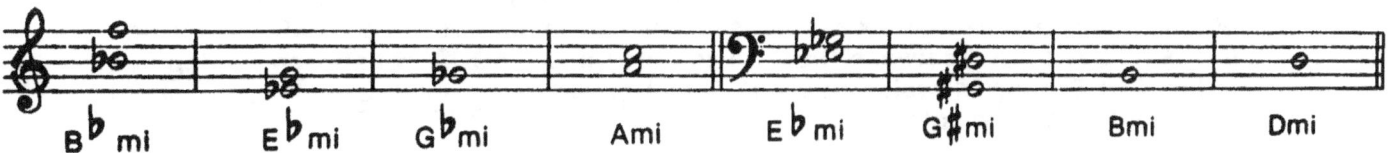

Bbmi Ebmi Gbmi Ami Ebmi G#mi Bmi Dmi

Exercise 3. Write these Minor Triads.

Dbmi Bmi Emi Gmi F#mi Emi Ami Cmi

DEGREE NAMES

Each note of the scale can be referred to by a degree number and a corresponding **DEGREE NAME**. They are as follows:

- I — TONIC
- II — SUPERTONIC
- III — MEDIANT
- IV — SUBDOMINANT
- V — DOMINANT
- VI — SUBMEDIANT
- VII — LEADING TONE
- VIII — UPPER TONIC

INVERSIONS

The original position of the chord is called the ROOT POSITION.

To invert means to turn upside down. A Triad can be inverted twice. Move the lowest note (Root Note) of the chord up an octave so that it becomes the top note of the chord. This is the FIRST INVERSION of the chord.

Next, move the lowest note of the First Inversion chord up an octave so it now becomes the top note of the chord. This is the SECOND INVERSION of the chord.

C MAJOR TRIAD

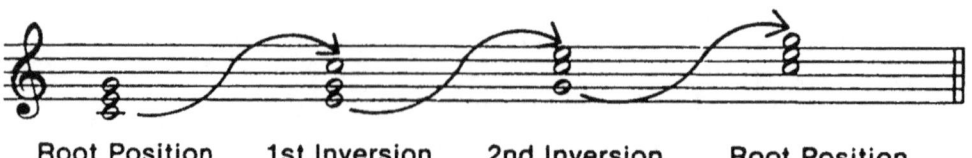

Root Position   1st Inversion   2nd Inversion   Root Position

The Inversions of a chord can easily be recognised by the intervals between the notes. The Root Position always consists of two thirds above each other. The First Inversion has a third between the 1st two notes and **a FOURTH between the top two notes.** The Second Inversion has a **FOURTH between the 1st two notes** and a third between the top two notes.

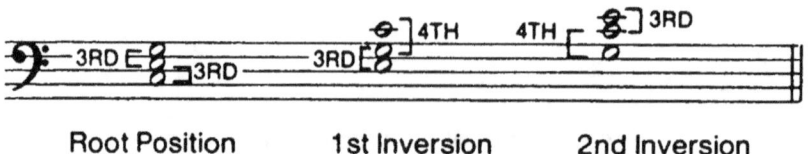

Root Position   1st Inversion   2nd Inversion

The Root Note of the chord is found at the **bottom** of a Root Position triad, at the **top** of a triad in the First Inversion and in the **middle** of a triad in the Second Inversion.

FIGURING

The distances between the notes can be also counted from the lowest note. Thus
the Root Position would have a 3rd and a 5th.
the 1st Inversion would have a 3rd and a 6th.
the 2nd Inversion would have a 4th and a 6th.

These distances can be used as a shorthand to indicate the inversion of a chord. The standard procedure is to place these numbers next to the degree number of the chord.

Thus: I_3^5 I_3^6 I_4^6

This procedure is known as 'Figuring'.

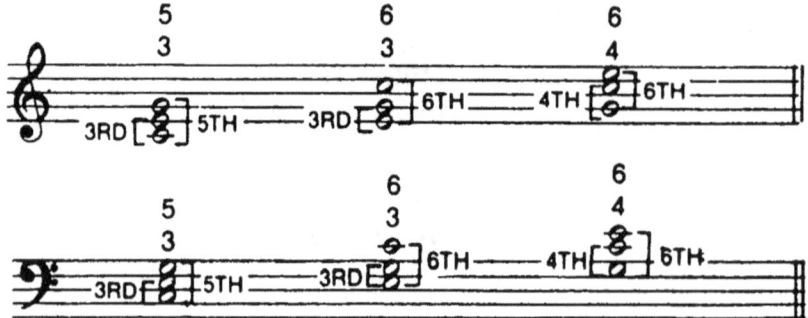

Generally the numbers of the Root Position are understood and only the degree number will appear. Likewise the 3rd is understood in the First Inversion chord. Both numbers must be written however for the Second Inversion chord.

Thus: Root Position I

1st Inversion I^6

2nd Inversion I$^6_4$

This shorthand system is found in music from the 15th Century onwards. In sheet music and modern chord charts of popular music the inversion of a chord is indicated by writing the actual name of the lowest note of the chord under the chord symbol.

Thus C Major Chord in the First Inversion would be written $^C/_E$. This means play C chord over an E Bass Note. The sound of the chord is dominated by the lowest sounding note so that no matter which arrangement the other notes are in, the chord will still produce the sound of a First Inversion chord.

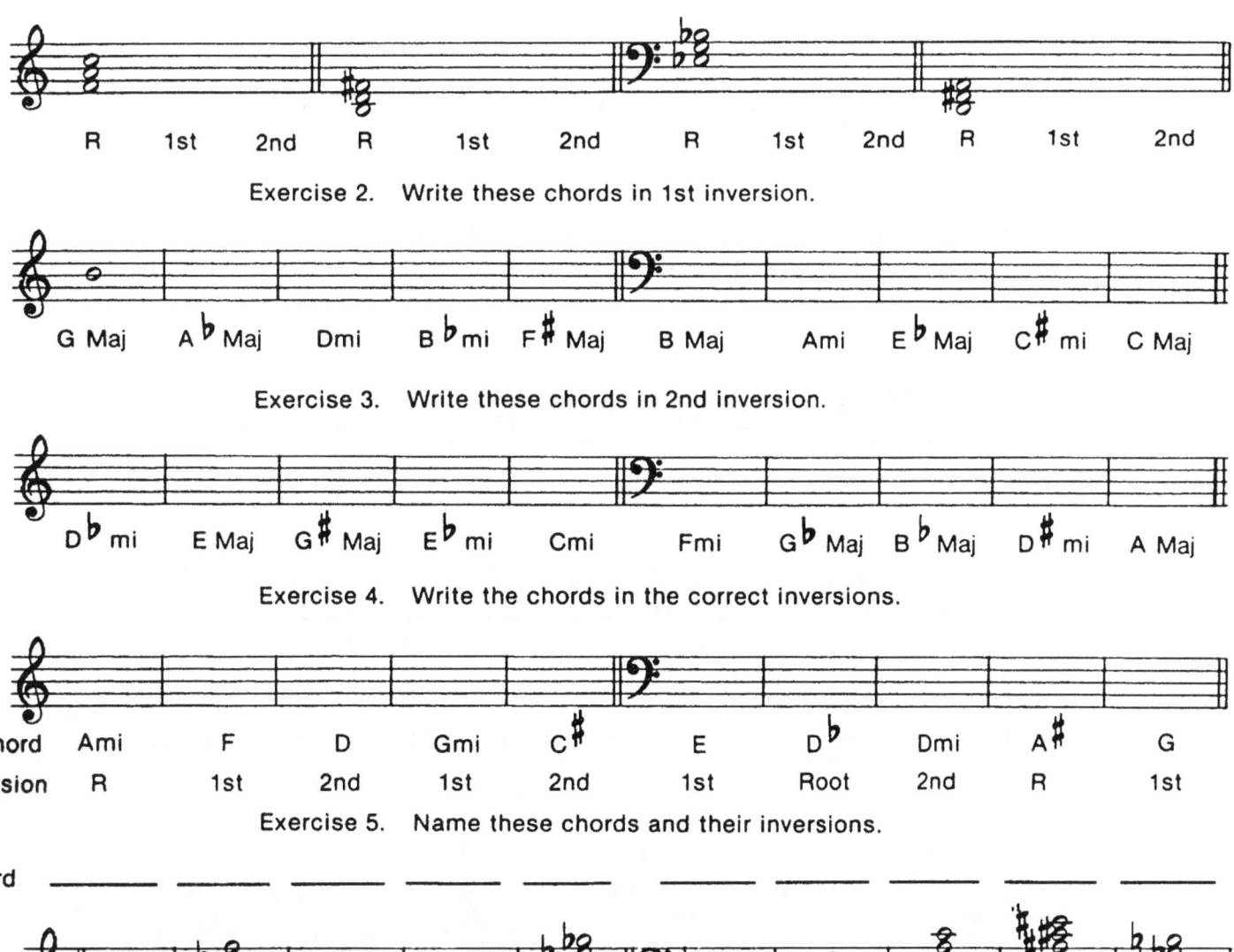

THE DIMINISHED TRIAD

The word 'diminish' means to make **smaller.** The triad is therefore made up of the smallest building-block units.

These are the ways to work out a Diminished Triad.

(1) Using **Semitones**: the distance between each of the notes is 3 semitones.

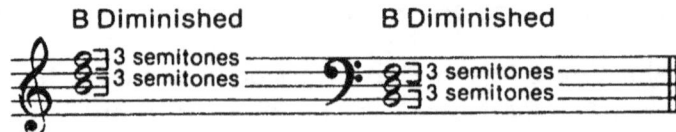

(2) Using **Minor 3rds**: the Diminished triad is made up of 2 minor thirds (the smallest thirds.).

(3) Using **Intervals**: Build a minor third from the Root Note and add to it a Diminished 5th interval.

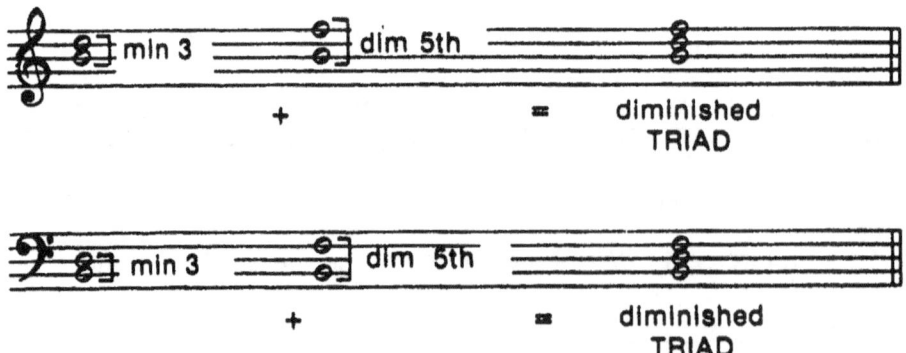

(4) From the **Major Chord**: Lower both the 3rd and 5th degrees by a semitone.

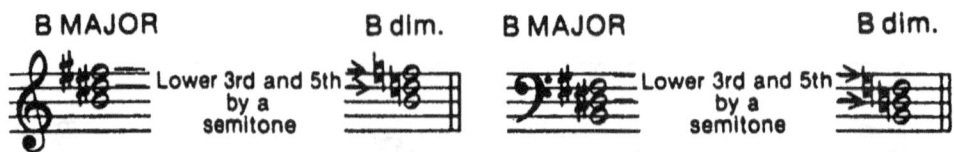

A Diminished Triad is indicated by its letter name followed by a small circle. Thus F#°

Exercise 1. Complete these Diminished triads in Root Position.

Exercise 2. Write these Diminished Triads in the correct inversion.

Exercise 3. Write Diminished Triads below the given notes and indicate the inversions.

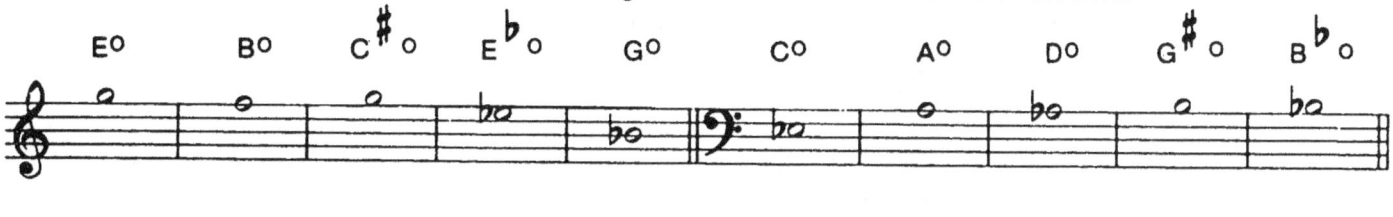

REVIEW

Exercise 4. Name the following chords in the spaces provided above, and indicate the inversion in the spaces provided below.

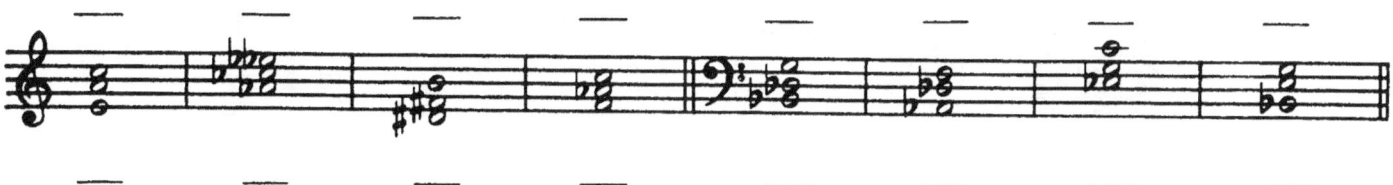

Exercise 5. Write the chords asked for, in close position, in the inversion indicated by the figuring.

THE AUGMENTED TRIAD

The word 'Augment' means to make larger. The Triad is therefore made up of the largest building-block units.

These are the ways to work out an Augmented Triad.

(1) Using **Semitones**: the distance between each of the notes is 4 semitones.

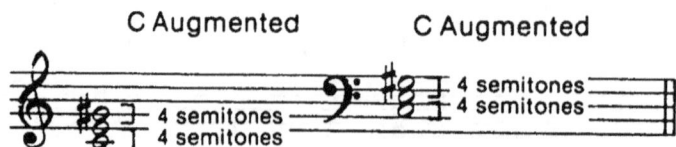

(2) Using **Major 3rds**: the Augmented triad is made up of 2 Major 3rds. (the largest 3rds used in chord building.)

(3) Using **Intervals**: Build a Major 3rd from the root note and add to it an Augmented 5th interval.

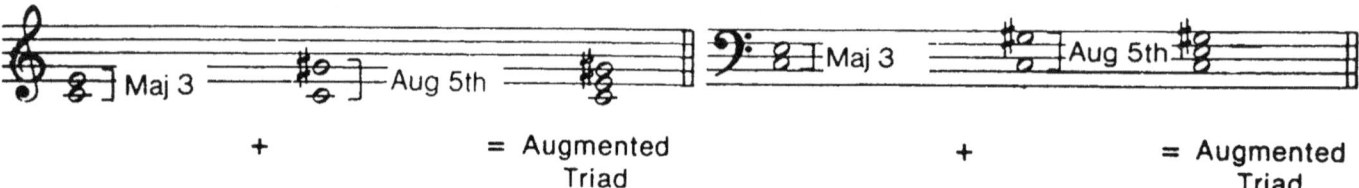

(4) From the **Major chord**: Raise the 5th degree by a semitone.

IMPORTANT NOTE: There are twelve semitones in the octave and the building-blocks of 4 semitones and the Major 3rd therefore divide evenly into the Octave. As a result, there are only '4' Augmented Chords.

For instance C Augmented Chord (C.E.G♯) when inverted once is exactly the same as E Augmented Chord (E.G♯.B♯). Remember that B♯ is the same note as C.

Work out the Augmented chords on any four consecutive semitones and write them in all inversions and the result will be all the possible Augmented chords.

The way you name the Triad will depend on the way it is written. Make sure you find the Root Position shape and then name the chord in relation to its lowest note.

The Augmented triad is indicated by its letter name followed by a small plus sign. Thus: G+.

Exercise 1. Complete the following Augmented Triads in Root Position.

Exercise 2. Write the following Augmented Triads in the correct inversions.

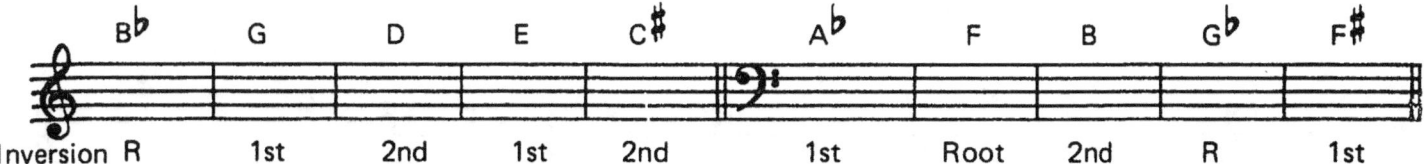

Exercise 3. Write the following Augmented Triads below the given notes and indicate the inversions.

Inversion _____ _____ _____ _____ _____ _____ _____ _____ _____ _____

Exercise 4. Write Augmented Triads and their inversions on the notes called for.
Give the enharmonic names for the inversions.

Exercise 5. Change these Major Triads (a) to Diminished Triads
&(b) to Augmented Triads

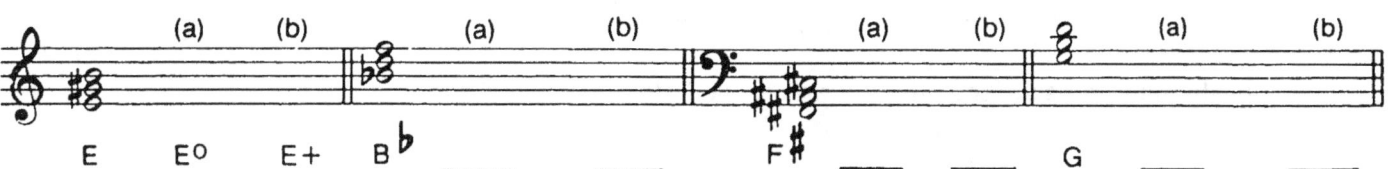

Exercise 6. Name these triads and their inversions.

NAME _____ _____ _____ _____ _____ _____ _____ _____ _____ _____

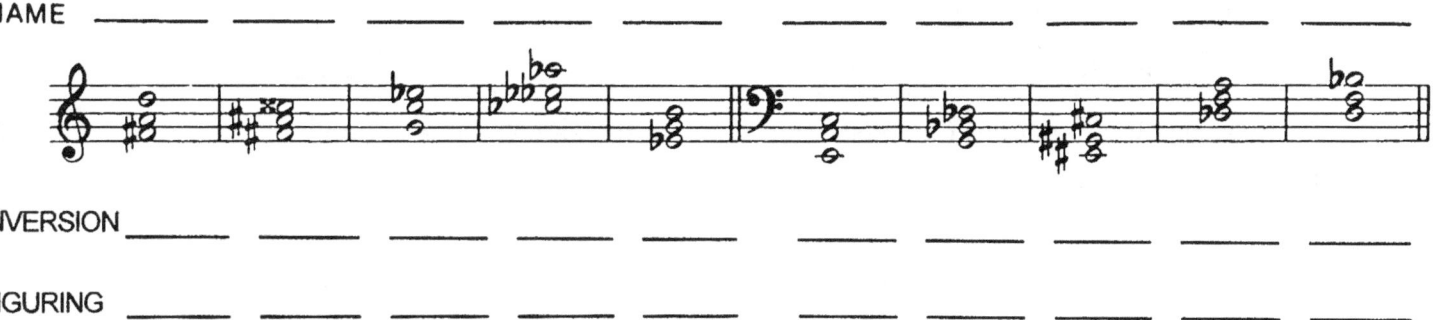

INVERSION _____ _____ _____ _____ _____ _____ _____ _____ _____ _____

FIGURING _____ _____ _____ _____ _____ _____ _____ _____ _____ _____

21

WHERE TO FIND MAJOR, MINOR, DIMINISHED & AUGMENTED TRIADS

Below are the scales of C Major and A Minor in all forms. A Triad has been built on every note of these scales. Name all the triads.

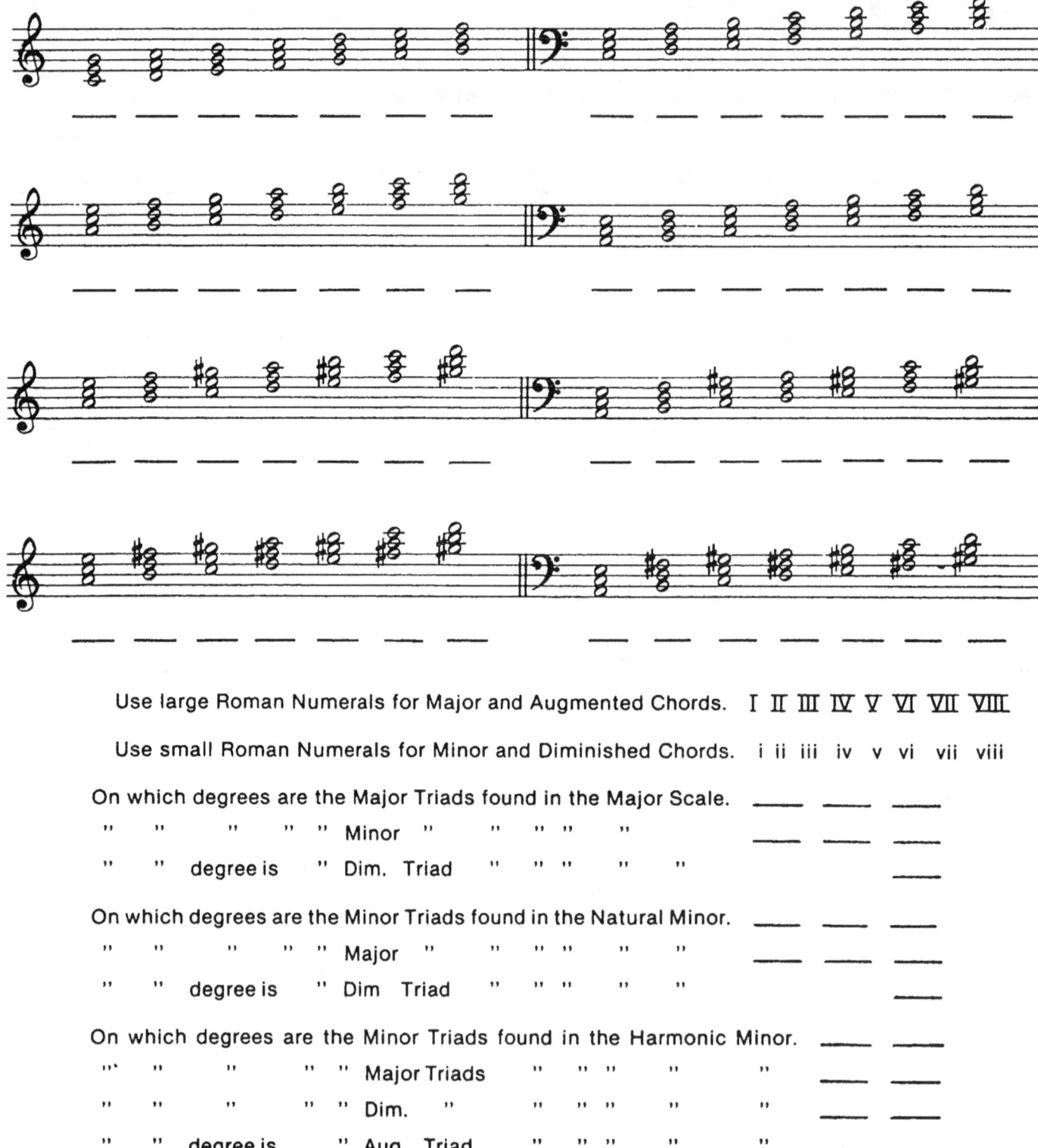

Use large Roman Numerals for Major and Augmented Chords.   I II III IV V VI VII VIII

Use small Roman Numerals for Minor and Diminished Chords.   i ii iii iv v vi vii viii

On which degrees are the Major Triads found in the Major Scale.   _____ _____ _____
   "   "   "   "   " Minor "   " " "   _____ _____ _____
   "   " degree is " Dim. Triad " " " " "   _____

On which degrees are the Minor Triads found in the Natural Minor.   _____ _____ _____
   "   "   "   " " Major "   " " " "   _____ _____ _____
   "   " degree is " Dim Triad " " " " "   _____

On which degrees are the Minor Triads found in the Harmonic Minor.   _____ _____
   "*   "   "   " " Major Triads " " " " "   _____ _____
   "   "   "   " " Dim. " " " " " "   _____ _____
   "   " degree is   " Aug. Triad " " " " "   _____

In the ascending form only, (the descending form is the same as the Natural).
On which degrees are the Minor Triads found in the Melodic Minor.   _____ _____
   "   "   "   " " Major Triads " " " " "   _____ _____
   "   "   "   " " Dim.Triads " " " " "   _____ _____
   "   " degree is   " Aug. Triad " " " " "   _____

CHORD TABLES

The chords on the previous page can be organised into a table of chords for Major Keys and Minor Keys.

The Major Chord Table is arranged thus:—

<u>C MAJOR</u>

IV	I	V
F	C	G
ii	vi	iii
Dmi	Ami	Emi
		vii°
		B°

When arranged in this manner it can be easily seen as part of the cycle of fifths. (See Page 4). The relative minor chords are placed underneath the Major Chords. The Diminished chord is placed under the Vth degree as it functions in much the same way as the Vth.

The Minor Chord Table is a selection of the most used chords in a piece of minor music. It must be borne in mind however that all the chords that are built on all the forms of the minor scale are likely to occur in the pieces.

The Minor Chord Table is arranged thus:—

<u>A MINOR</u>

iv	i	V
Dmi	Ami	E
VI	III(+)	ii°
F	C	B°
		vii°
		G#°

Exercise 1.
Write the Chord Tables (both the degree numbers and the chord names) for G Major scale and G minor Scale.

<u>G MAJOR CHORD TABLE</u>

<u>G MINOR CHORD TABLE</u>

24

EXERCISES

The folowing questions are divided into four sections:

1. Work out the key of each line of music. The Key Signature and Final chord will confirm the key.
2. Write the Chord Table for the key. Be careful to use the Major Table or the Minor Table in accordance with your findings for 1.
3. Name all the chords, placing the chord symbols above the chords as shown in the example.
4. Place the Degree number and Figuring in the area below each chord, also as shown in the example.

HOW THE TRIADS FUNCTION

If the student has named the chords on page 22 correctly, he or she will have found that the Major and Minor chords are to be found on the Tonic notes of the Major and Minor scales, as well as several positions inbetween.

These chords have a static or resting feeling. By this I mean that they are good chords on which to end a section of music.

The Augmented and Diminished chords, however, are never found on the Tonic degree of the scale. They are chords of movement, which always lead on to a Major or Minor rest chord. They are known as LEADING FUNCTION chords.

The diminished chord is most often used in its position as the chord on the viith degree of the scale. It has a very strong pull (lead) back to the Tonic chord of the scale. (Play and listen to Example 1).

Example 1.

The Augmented chord is found on the IIIrd degree of the Harmonic Minor scale. When inverted once, it is the same chord as the Augmented chord on the Vth degree. It is most often used as a replacement for the usual Dominant Chord which is a Major chord. It provides an extra strong lead back to the Tonic Chord. (Play and listen to Example 2).

Example 2.

Exercise 1.

Write these chords in close position to each other, keeping the movement of the notes as small as possible. Start on varying inversions. Mark each chord as a Leading Function (L.F.) or Rest chord. (R). Follow the pattern given.

E.g.

Play the chords you have written and listen to the strong pull from the Leading Function Chords to the Rest Chords.

THE SUSPENDED 4TH TRIAD

There is one other triad in common use today. It is the Suspended 4th Triad. In this triad the 4th degree of the scale replaces the third. The sound this creates is one of being 'suspended' in mid-air. There is a strong downward pull. The chord usually resolves onto either a Major or minor triad as the 4th moves down to the third. As there is no third in the chord it is the same for Major and minor keys.

The sound is often used in church music. It is also a sound common to popular Rock and Jazz music, especially if the particular piece has its origin in Gospel music.

These are the easiest ways to work out a Suspended triad:—

(1) From the **Major** or **minor scale:** take the 1st, 4th and 5th notes.

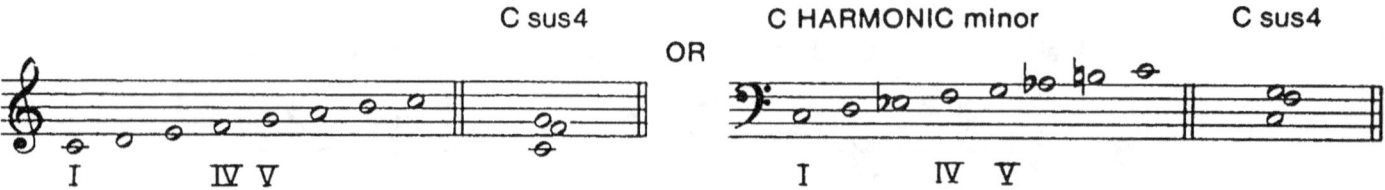

(2) Using **Intervals:** Build a Perfect 4th from the root note and add to it a Perfect 5th.

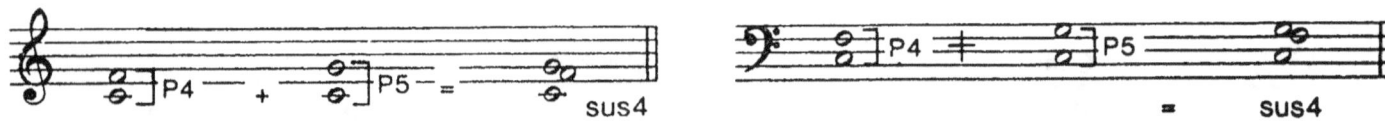

(3) **Building up from the root:** From the first note to the second note is a Perfect 4th and from the second note to the third is a Major 2nd.

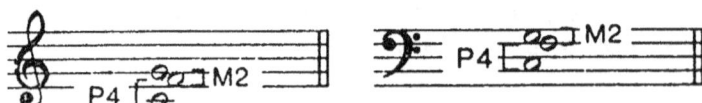

(4) From the **Major** or **minor chord:** replace the third degree with the 4th.

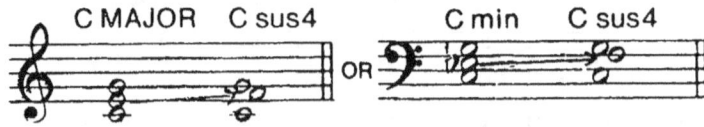

This chord would be classed as a leading function triad.

The chord symbol for a Suspended 4th Triad is either 'sus 4' or simply 'sus' the 4 being understood. e.g. Fsus4 or Fsus.

Exercise 1. Complete these Suspended 4th Triads in Root Position.

Exercise 2. Write these Suspended 4th Triads with their inversions.

Exercise 3. Name these triads. **Indicate the inversions.**

NAME ____ ____ ____ ____ ____ ____ ____ ____ ____ ____

INV. ____ ____ ____ ____ ____ ____ ____ ____ ____ ____

Exercise 4. Write Major, minor, diminished, Augmented and Suspended 4th Triads in Root Position on these notes.

Exercise 5. Using D as the top note of each chord write the appropriate inversions of these chords:

INV. ____ ____ ____ ____ ____   ____ ____ ____ ____ ____   ____ ____ ____ ____ ____

Exercise 6. Using Ab as the top note of each chord, write the appropriate inversions of these chords:

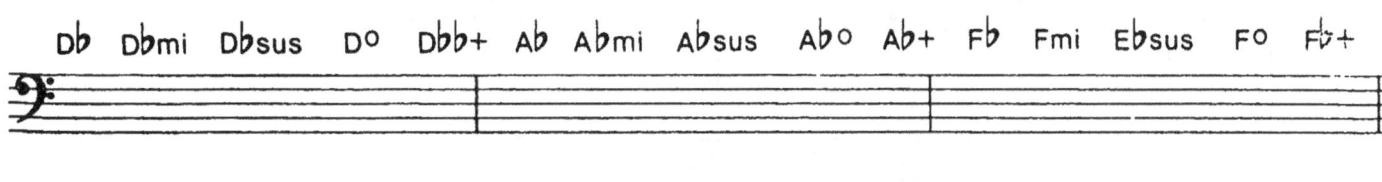

INV. ____ ____ ____ ____ ____   ____ ____ ____ ____ ____   ____ ____ ____ ____ ____

28 Fill in the triads below (harmonise) each of these melody notes. Do not harmonise those notes marked *

The same chord notes will continue over one or more bars until another chord change symbol appears.

MELLOW WALTZ

M.S. BRANDMAN

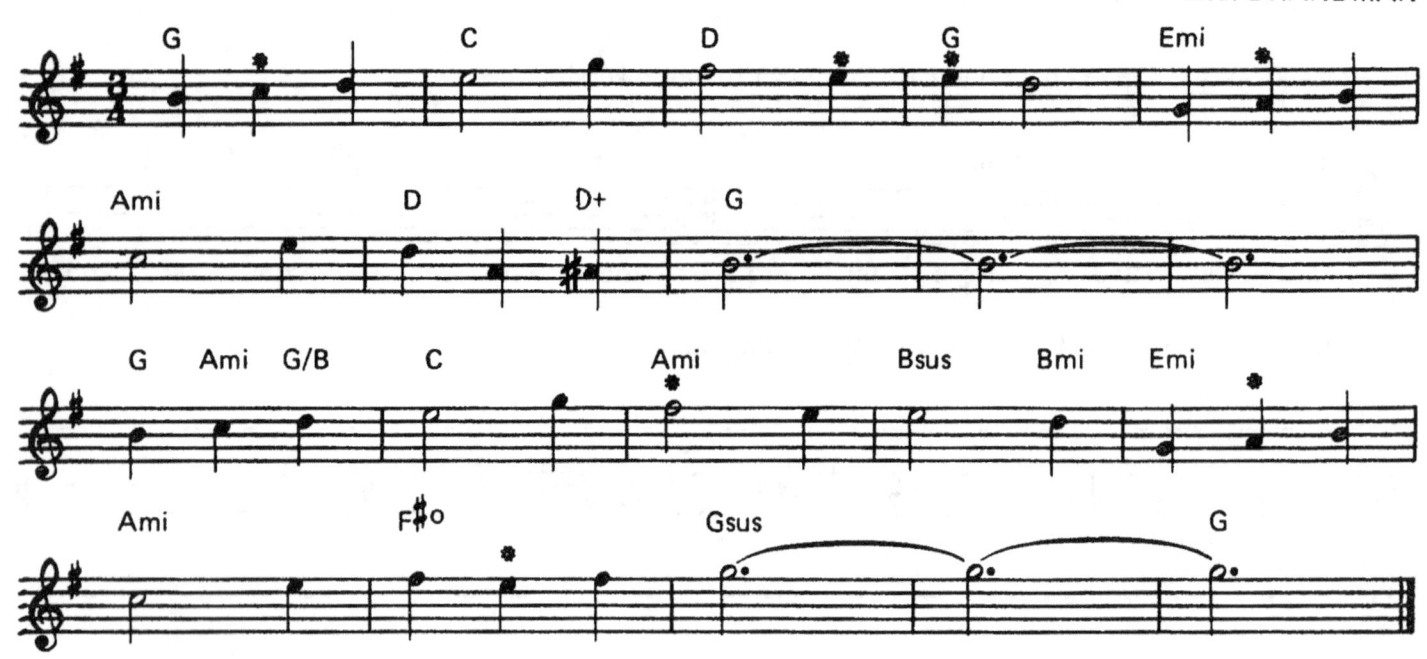

ACCOMPANIMENT

STYLE 1)

To provide a Left Hand piano accompaniment to the tune, play the Root Note of the chord in the lower register (area) of the keyboard (Below ) and play two chords on the 2nd and 3rd beats of the bar, in the middle area of the piano. (Above).

If there are two bars of the same chord, follow the same procedure, but play the Dominant Note (Vth) as the lower Bass note in the second bar.

If there are three chords per bar, play the Root Note or which ever Bass notes are marked under the chord names, as **single notes only** in the lower register of the keyboard.

STYLE 2)

An alternative style of Left Hand accompaniment is to play one chord lasting the length of the bar (in this case a dotted minim's value) in the middle register of the keyboard.

THE MODES

Our present day scales — Major and Natural Minor, evolved from the seven modes, used in Church Music from the 13th Century onwards. Each of these modes can be represented by a white note scale on the piano.

The Modal Name of the C Major Scale — all the white notes from C to C, is the Ionian Mode. The Mode on the white notes from D to D is the Dorian Mode. The others are:—

> Phrygian Mode — from E to E
> Lydian Mode — from F to F
> Mixolydian Mode — from G to G
> Aeolian Mode — from A to A
> Locrian Mode — from B to B

Each of the Modal Scales is constructed of a different arrangement of tones and semitones.

MODAL SOUNDS

Positive or Major Sounding Modes

(1) LYDIAN (2) IONIAN (3) MIXOLYDIAN

Mode of Median Stability

DORIAN (Halfway between Major and minor)

Negative or minor Sounding Modes

(1) AEOLIAN (2) PHRYGIAN (3) LOCRIAN

Modes are useful to know, as each scale can be seen as the PARENT Scale of a type of Chord. (Just as the Major Scale is the PARENT Scale of the Major Triad).

The chords in the next section of the book can be seen in two ways:—
(1) In relation to the Major or minor Scale (whichever is applicable).
OR (2) As the Tonic chord of a Mode.

Refer to *Contemporary Theory Workbook – Book 2 Part B*
Complete Lessons 1-10 before commencing this section.

THE MODES (and how to find them)

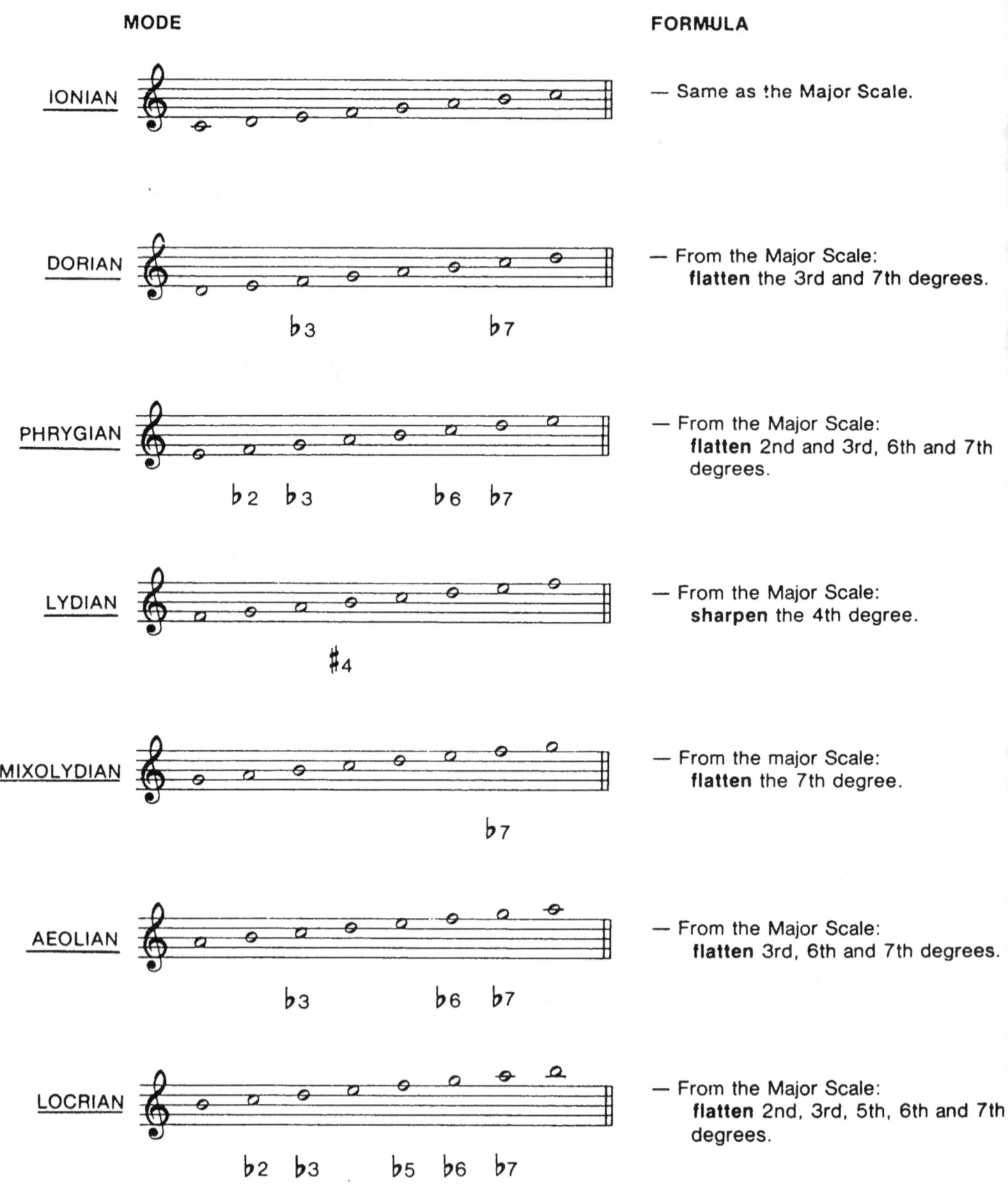

Complete TWO sections to this question.

1. Write the Modes called for, starting on either C (Treble Clef exercises) or A (Bass Clef exercises). Use Accidentals.

2. Collate the resulting accidentals into the form of a Key Signature in the space provided, and state to which MAJOR key the Key Signature belongs. (This information should provide you with an alternate manner with which to find the Modal scales.)

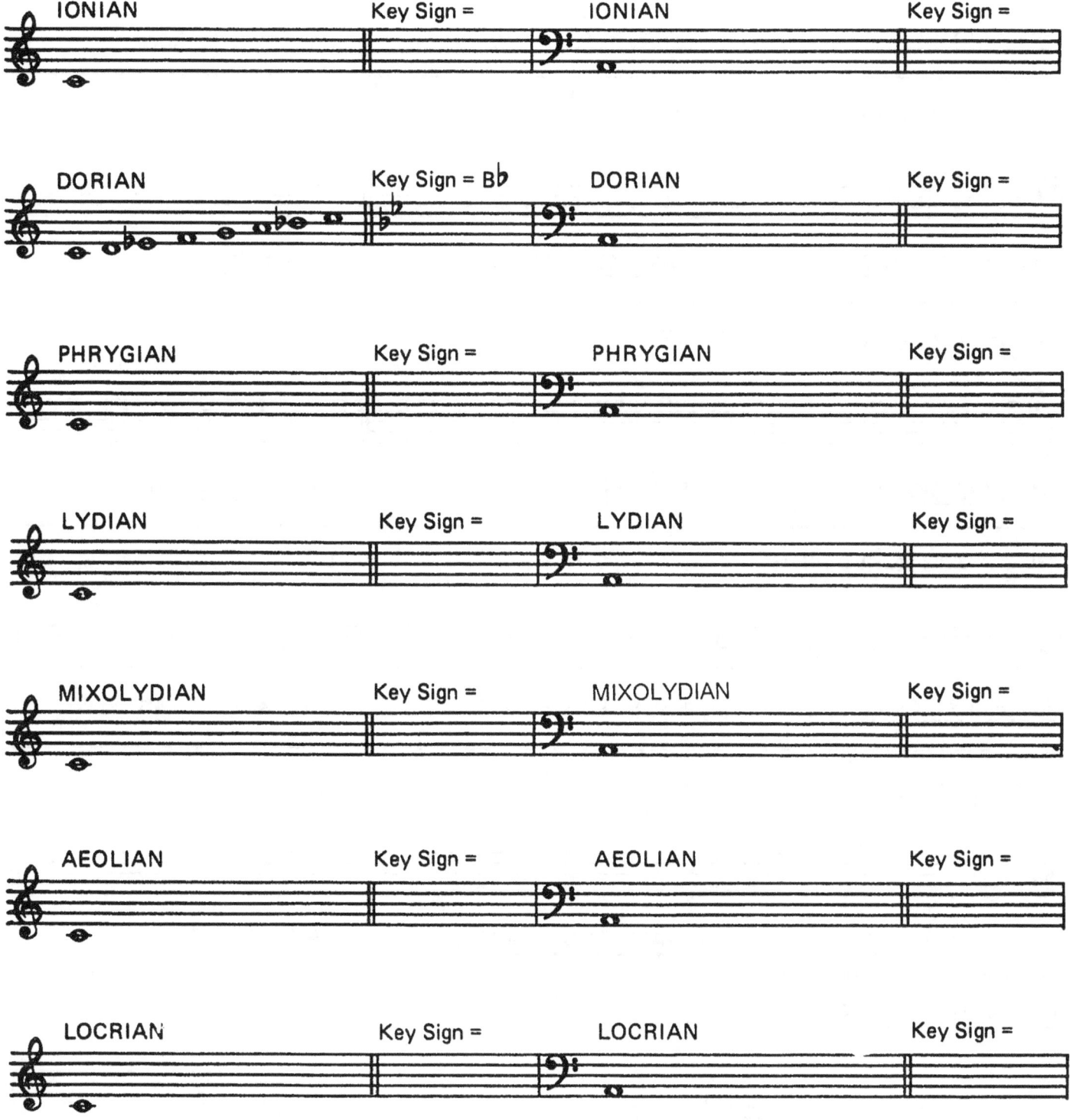

32. Complete TWO sections to this question.
   1. Write the MODES on the notes called for. Use **accidentals**.
   2. Write in the names of the Major scales which have the same key signature as the Modes you have written. For instance: The Dorian Mode on E will have 2 sharps, F sharp and C Sharp. These sharps belong to the Key signature of 'D Major' scale.

DORIAN MODES ON: D   B   E♭

SAME KEY SIGN AS '___'   SAME KEY SIGN AS '___'   SAME KEY SIGN AS '___'

PHRYGIAN MODES ON: E   C   D♯

SAME KEY SIGN AS '___'   SAME KEY SIGN AS '___'   SAME KEY SIGN AS '___'

LYDIAN MODES ON: F   A♭   A

SAME KEY SIGN AS '___'   SAME KEY SIGN AS '___'   SAME KEY SIGN AS '___'

MIXOLYDIAN MODES ON: G   D♭   E

SAME KEY SIGN AS '___'   SAME KEY SIGN AS '___'   SAME KEY SIGN AS '___'

AEOLIAN MODES ON: A   F   B

SAME KEY SIGN AS '___'   SAME KEY SIGN AS '___'   SAME KEY SIGN AS '___'

LOCRIAN MODES ON: B   C   G♯

SAME KEY SIGN AS '___'   SAME KEY SIGN AS '___'   SAME KEY SIGN AS '___'

SEVENTH CHORDS

33

A Seventh Chord is one that combines the 1st, 3rd, 5th and 7th notes from the Root. Seventh Chords can be built on every note of the Major and Minor scales.

DOMINANT SEVENTH CHORDS

The Dominant Seventh Chord is the most frequently used seventh chord. It has a strong leading function bringing about a resolution onto the Tonic Chord of the scale. When seventh chords are built on each note of the scale, the first chord is known as the Tonic 7th chord, the second as the Supertonic seventh and so on. As the **fifth degree** is known as the **Dominant** note, the seventh built on that note must be the **Dominant Seventh chord.**

Below are the sevenths built on each note of the Major and Harmonic Minor scales.

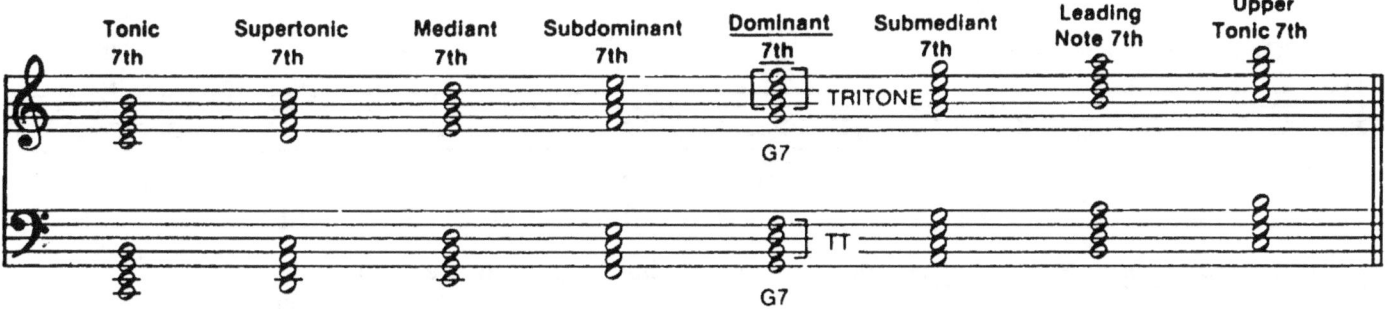

*TT = Tritone

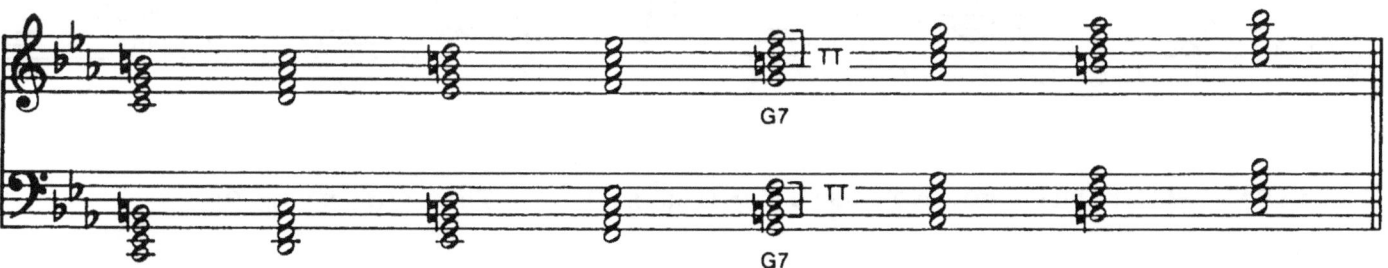

In the Keys of C major and C minor, the Dominant Seventh chord is G7th (G.B.D.F.). The 7th chord leads back to either the C major or C minor triad. (In the Harmonic Minor scale, the Dominant seventh chord is the same as that in the Major scale, owing to the use of the Raised 7th in this form of the Minor scale).

The key component of the chord, that provides this very strong pull, is the interval of a TRITONE (3 tones) between the notes B and F. The interval can also be seen as an Augmented 4th or a Diminished 5th. It is also present in the diminished triad, (see page 18) and is the reason why it too, has a strong leading function. The notes of the Tritone, (B and F) pull very strongly by a semitone to the notes C and E (or Eb in the minor chord).

WAYS TO WORK OUT A DOMINANT SEVENTH CHORD

(1) From the **Major Scale:** Build a seventh chord on the Vth degree. (1.3.5.7.).

(2) From the **Harmonic Minor Scale:** Build a seventh chord on the Vth degree.

(3) Using a **Mode:** Build a seventh chord on the Ist degree of the Mixolydian Mode. (Thus the Mixolydian Mode becomes the scale of the Dominant seventh chord).

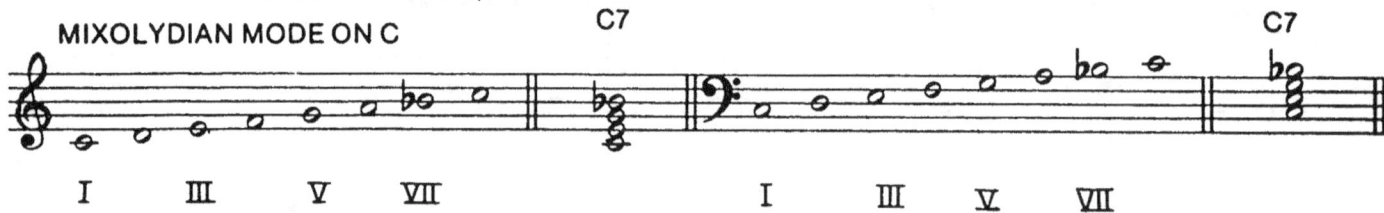

(4) Using **Major** and **Minor thirds** and semitones: Build up from the Root note, using a Major third (4 semitones) then a minor third (3 semitones) and another minor third (3 semitones).

(5) Using **Intervals:** From the Root Note use a Major Third, a Perfect Fifth, and a Minor 7th.

(6) From a **Major Chord:** Add a Minor Seventh interval from the Root Note to the chord.

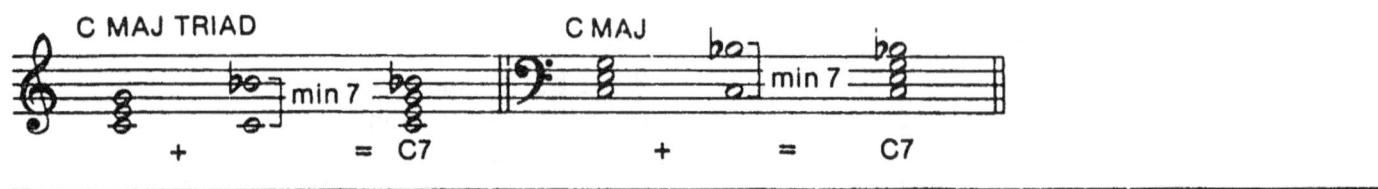

The symbol for the Dominant Seventh chord is simply the number '7'.
The word 'dominant' is taken to be understood owing to the frequent use of the chord.

(1) Complete these Dominant 7th chords.

    G7   B7   D♭7   F7   A7   C7   E7   G♭7   B♭7   D7

(2) Write these Dominant 7th chords.

    F♯7   B♭7   C7   E7   G♯7   A♭7   D7   C♯7   G7   E♭7

(3) Name these Dominant 7th chords and state to which keys they belong.

NAME: F7 _____ _____ _____ _____ _____ _____ _____ _____ _____

KEY: B♭ or B♭mi _____

NAME: _____ _____ _____ _____ _____ _____ _____ _____ _____ _____

KEY: _____

(4) Resolve these Dominant seventh chords onto the nearest inversion of either the Tonic Major or Tonic Minor chord.

e.g. Root — 2nd

INVERSIONS OF SEVENTH CHORDS

As there is one extra note in a seventh chord (from the triad) there necessarily must be one extra inversion of a seventh chord. In all there are three inversions in addition to the Root Position.

Following the method of inverting a chord shown on page 12, the inversions of a seventh chord will always follow this format:—

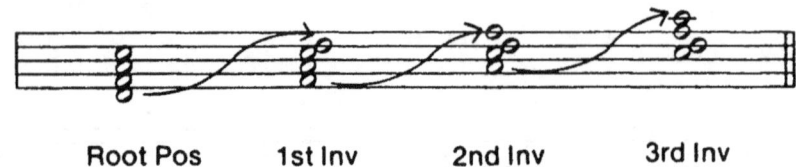

Root Pos   1st Inv   2nd Inv   3rd Inv

Once again, the inversions of a seventh (as with the inversions of a triad) can easily be recognised by the distinctive shape of each chord and the intervals between each note.

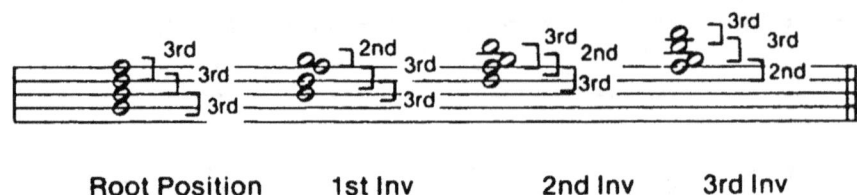

Root Position   1st Inv   2nd Inv   3rd Inv

The distances between the notes can also be counted from the lowest note.
Thus the intervals from the lowest note in the Root Position are: 3rd, 5th & 7th.
    "   "   "   "   "   "   "   "   "   1st Inversion   " 3rd, 5th & 6th.
    "   "   "   "   "   "   "   "   "   2nd Inversion   " 3rd, 4th & 6th.
    "   "   "   "   "   "   "   "   "   3rd Inversion   " 2nd, 4th & 6th.

NB. Arrow marks the Root note.

From these intervals, the 'figuring' for 7th chords is taken. Below are the 'figures' for the Root Position and inversions of the 7ths. The numbers which are understood are in brackets.

Root Pos.	1st Inv.	2nd Inv.	3rd Inv.
7	6	(6)	(6)
(5)	5	4	4
(3)	(3)	3	2

Thus the standard figuring for the above is:—

Root Pos.	1st Inv.	2nd Inv.	3rd Inv.
7	6	4	4
	5	3	2

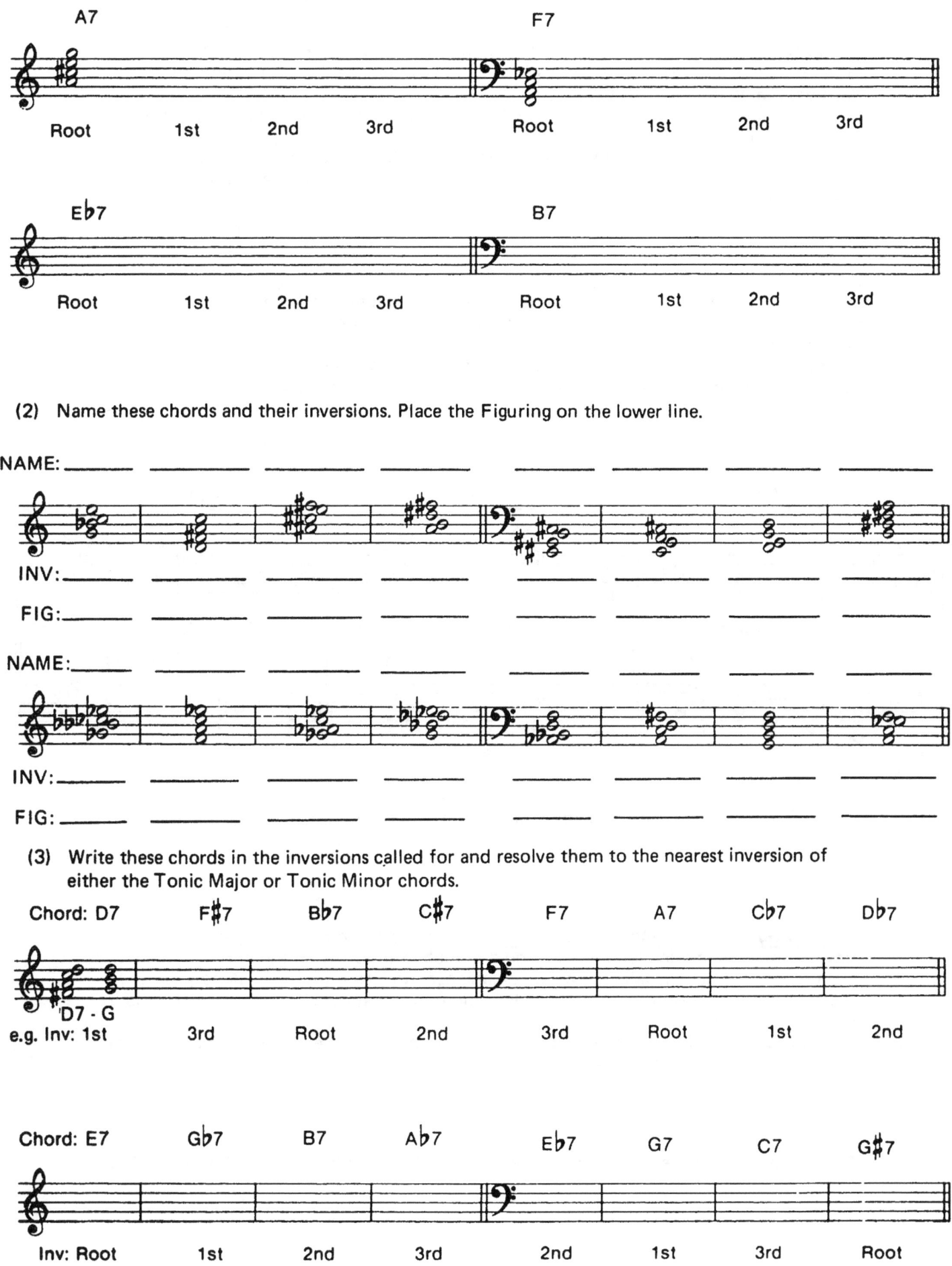

DIMINISHED SEVENTH CHORDS

This chord is an extension of the diminished triad. A diminished 7th interval is added to the diminished triad. It is found as the 7th chord built on the viith degree of the Harmonic Minor scale. (See page 6).

It is a leading function chord and it will resolve in the same way as the Diminished triad, onto the Root Chord of the Key.

Although it is found in the Minor scale only, it is often used as a borrowed chord in the Major Key. It can therefore lead back to the Tonic Major chord as well as the Tonic Minor chord.

SPECIAL NOTE

As each note in the Diminished Seventh chord is equidistant from the next, and because there are 12 semitones in the octave, there are only '3' diminished seventh chord shapes.

They can be written 12 different ways, but the notes on the keyboard, or any other instrument for that matter, will always conform to one of these three basic shapes.

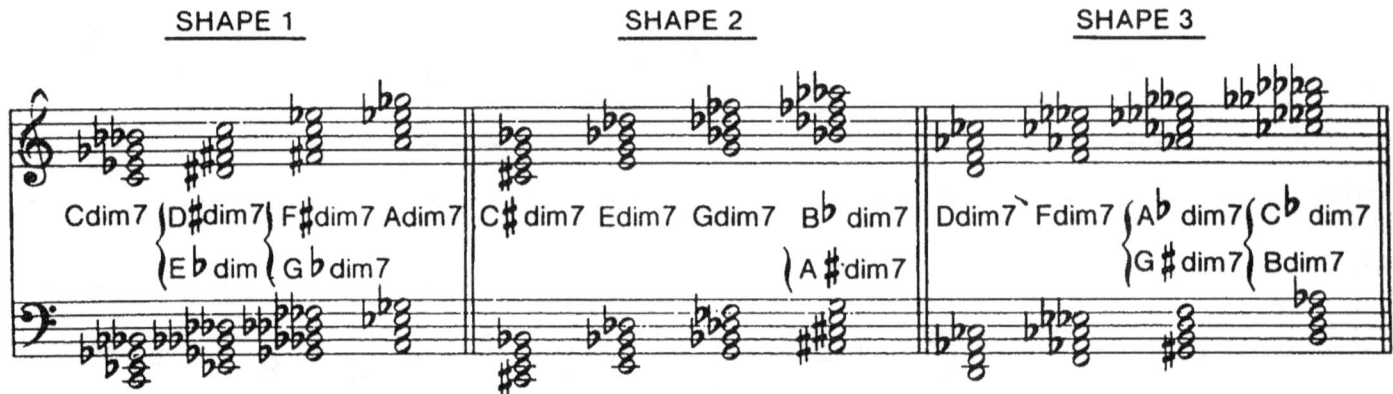

N.B. Brackets indicate the same chord written enharmonically. (See page 1).

The symbol for a diminished 7th chord is either the circle or 'dim 7'. As seen previously, the circle is also used for the diminished triad. When the circle is used in sheet music it is usually taken to mean 'diminished 7th'. You will have to use your taste and harmonic knowledge to decide whether the chord that best suits the situation is a triad or a seventh.

For the purposes of this book, use the symbol 'dim 7' to name these chords and leave the circle (º) for the diminished triad.

For information on the Diminished Scale, refer to the Appendix in Book 2 of this series.

WAYS TO WORK OUT A DIMINISHED 7TH CHORD

(1) From the **Harmonic Minor scale:** Build a Seventh chord on the viith degree.

(2) Using **minor 3rds** (3 semitones ea): Build up from the Root Note using a minor 3rd, minor 3rd and another minor 3rd.

(3) Using **Intervals:** From the Root Note use a Minor 3rd, a diminished 5th and a diminished seventh.

(4) From a **Diminished triad:** add a diminished seventh interval from the Root note, to the triad
OR: add another minor 3rd on top.

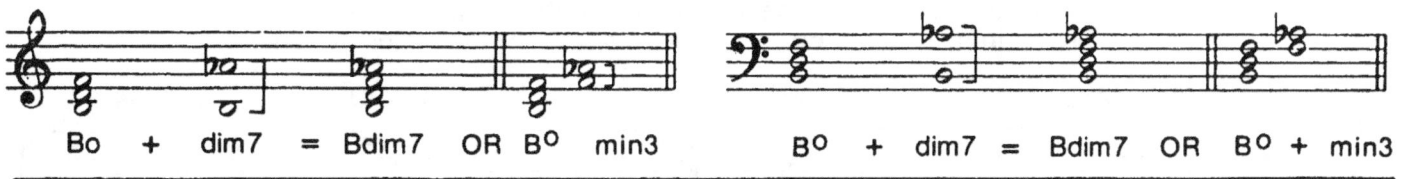

EXERCISES

(1) Complete these Diminished 7th chords in Root Position.

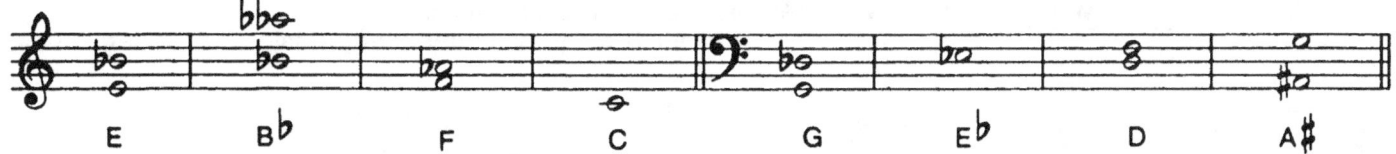

(2) Write these Diminished 7th chords and their inversions. Give the alternate names for the inversions.

C♯dim7 ___ ___ ___   G♯dim7 ___ ___ ___   F♯dim7 ___ ___ ___   Bdim7 ___ ___ ___

R   1st   2nd   3rd   R   1st   2nd   3rd   R   1st   2nd   3rd   R   1st   2nd   3rd

(3) Mark which shape these Diminished 7th chords belong to: 1, 2 or 3.

SHAPE:___ ___ ___ ___ ___ ___ ___ ___

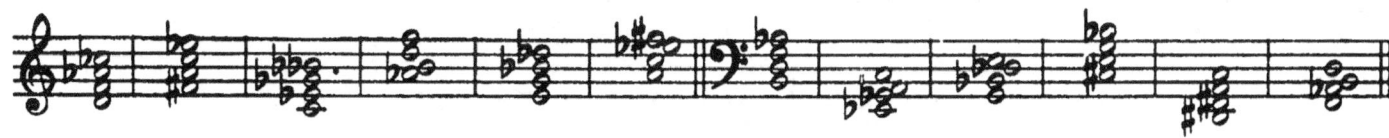

MAJOR SEVENTH CHORDS

The Major Seventh chord is usually found in its position as the Tonic Seventh chord of the Major scale. However it can also occur as the Subdominant Seventh chord of the Major Scale, or the Submediant chord of the Minor scale, (any form). (See page 22).
The chord functions as a 'rest' chord.

WAYS TO WORK OUT A MAJOR 7TH CHORD

(1) From the **Major Scale:** Build a seventh on the Tonic degree,
OR: build a seventh on the Subdominant degree.

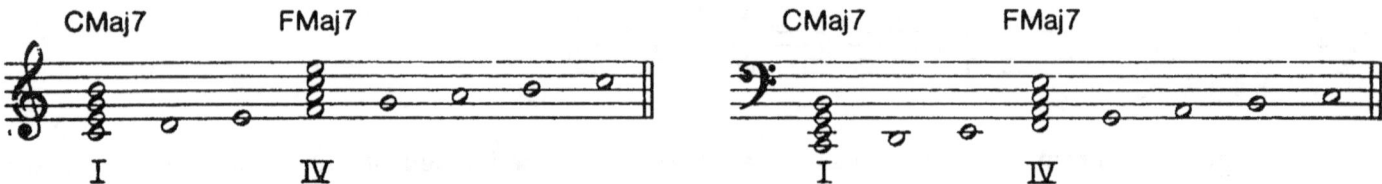

(2) From the **Minor Scale:** Build a seventh on the Submediant degree.

(3) From the **Modes:** Build a seventh on the 1st degree of the Ionian Mode,
OR: build a seventh on the 1st degree of the Lydian Mode.
Thus both scales can be regarded as scales of the Major 7th chord.

(4) Using **Major** and **Minor 3rds** and semitones: Build up from the Root Note using a Major 3rd (4 semitones), a Minor 3rd (3 semitones) and a Major 3rd (4 semitones).

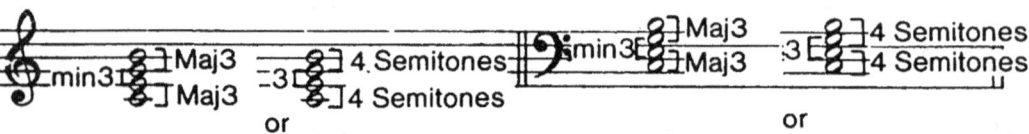

(5) Using **Intervals:** From the Root Note use a Major 3rd, a Perfect 5th and a Major 7th.

(6) From the **Major Chord:** Add a Major Seventh interval from the Root note to the chord.

The symbol for a Major Seventh chord is either 'Maj7' or 'Ma7'.

(1) Complete these Major Seventh chords in Root Position.

(2) Write all the inversions of these Major seventh chords.

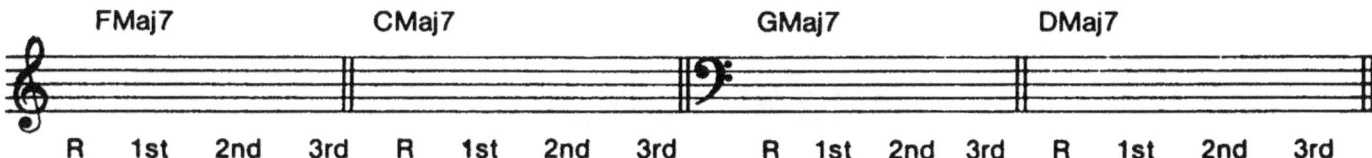

(3) Name these Major 7th chords and indicate the inversions.

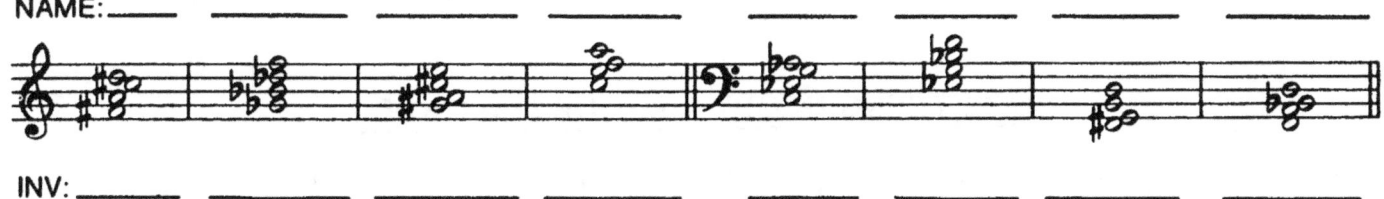

(4) Write these Major sevenths in the inversion called for.

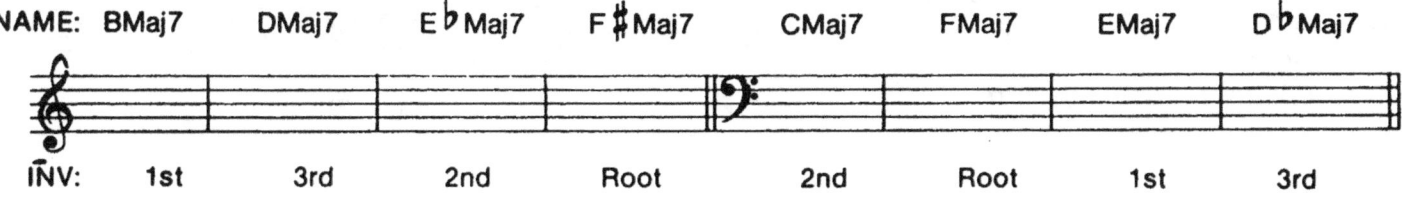

(5) Name the following chords as either Dominant 7ths (7), Diminished 7ths (dim 7) or Major 7ths (Maj 7) and indicate the inversion.

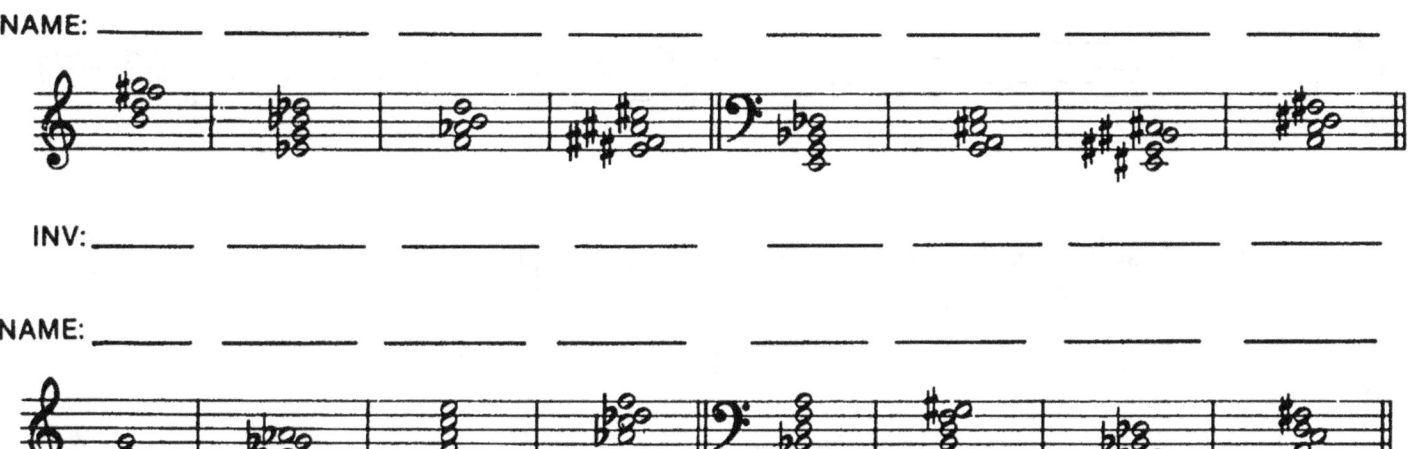

TWO-IN-ONE CHORDS
1a and 1b: Major 6th/Minor 7th

SIXTH CHORDS

A sixth chord is one that combines the 1st, 3rd, 5th and 6th notes from the Root Note. There are only two types of 6ths, the Major 6th and the Minor 6th and they occur only on specific notes of the Major and Minor scale. The other chords which look like 6ths are really only inversions of the seventh chords so far discussed. (i.e. the Dominant, Major and Diminished 7ths).

In classical terminology the chords are known as 'added 6th chords'.

(1a) THE MAJOR 6TH CHORD

The Major 6th chord can be found on either the Ist, IVth or Vth degree of the Major scale or on the VIth degree of the Harmonic Minor scale.

It is used as a 'rest' chord and therefore is a good chord to use either at the beginning or the end of a piece, as well as at various times during the piece.

WAYS TO WORK OUT A MAJOR 6TH CHORD

(1) From the **Major scale:** Build a sixth chord (1.3.5.6.) on either the Tonic (I), Subdominant (IV) or Dominant (V) degree.

(2) From the **Harmonic Minor:** Build a sixth chord on the Submediant (VI) degree.

(3) From the **Modes:** Build a sixth chord on the 1st degree of either the Ionian, Lydian or Mixolydian Mode.

(4) Using **Major** and **Minor 3rds, Major 2nds:** Build up from the Root Note using a
    Major 3rd (4 semitones), a Minor 3rd (3 semitones)
    and a Major 2nd (2 semitones).

(5) Using **Intervals:** From the Root Note use a Major 3rd, a Perfect 5th, and a Major 6th.

(6) From a **Major chord:** Add a Major 6th interval from the Root Note to the Major Chord.

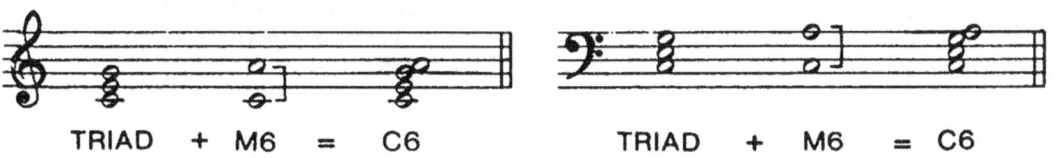

(7) From the **Minor 7th chord** (see next page): Use the 1st inversion.

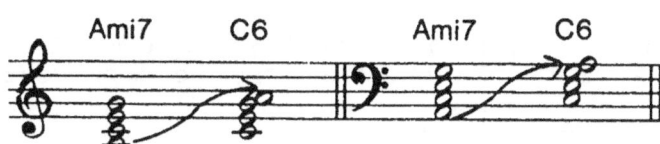

The symbol for a Major Sixth chord is simply the number '6', the word Major being understood.

---

(1) Complete the following Major 6th chords in Root Position.

(2) Write these Major 6th chords in all inversions. Mark the Major 2nds thus: ⌐

(3) Name these chords and mark the inversions.

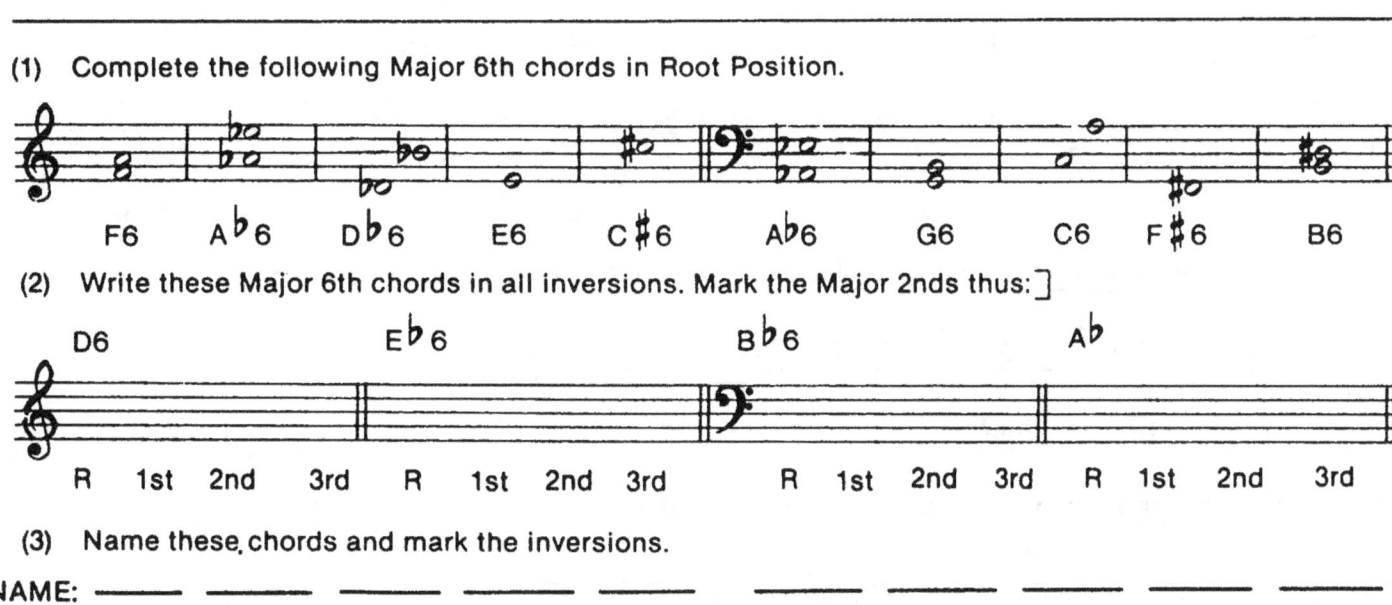

(1b) THE MINOR 7TH CHORD

When the Major 6th chord is inverted for the third time (3rd inversion) it in fact becomes another chord. This chord is known as a 'Minor 7th' chord owing to the fact that it is constructed of a Minor triad plus a Minor 7th interval from the Root Note.

It acts as a leading chord but the pull is not as strong as the leading function chords which contain the 'Tritone'. (See pages 14, 27 & 32.)

WAYS TO WORK OUT A MINOR 7TH CHORD

(1) From the **Major scale:** Build a seventh chord on either the Supertonic (II) Mediant (III) or Submediant (VI) degrees.

(2) From the **Modes:** Build a 7th chord on the 1st degree of either the Dorian, Phrygian or Aeolian (Natural Minor) Mode. (The Dorian Mode is regarded as the Mode best suited to the minor 7th chord).

(3) Using **Major and Minor 3rds:** Build up from the Root Note using a Minor 3rd (3 semitones), a Major 3rd (4 semitones) and a Minor 3rd (3 semitones).

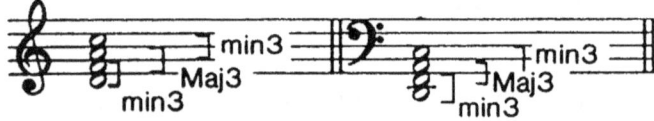

(4) Using **Intervals:** From the Root Note use a Minor 3rd, a Perfect 5th and a Minor 7th.

(5) From the **Minor triad:** Add a Minor 7th interval from the Root Note to the Minor triad.

(6) From a **Major 6th chord:** Use the 3rd inversion of the chord.

The chord symbol for a Minor 7th chord is 'mi7'.

MINOR 7TH CHORDS

(1) Complete the following Minor 7th chords in Root Position.

Ami7   Emi7   B♭mi7   Fmi7   D♭mi7   Dmi7   Fmi7   C♯mi7   G♭mi7   E♭mi7

(2) Write these Minor 7th chords in all inversions.

Cmi7 — R 1st 2nd 3rd   F♯mi7 — R 1st 2nd 3rd   Bmi7 — R 1st 2nd 3rd   A♭mi7 — R 1st 2nd 3rd

(3) Write these Major 6th chords and their equivalent Minor 7ths in Root Position.

e.g.

G6 = Emi7   B♭6 = ___   A♭6 = ___   D6 = ___

E6 = ___   D♭6 = ___   F♯6 = ___   B6 = ___

(4) Write these Minor 7th chords and their equivalent Major 6ths in Root Position.

e.g.

Dmi7 = F6   B♭mi7 ___   Ami7 ___   F♯mi7 ___

Bmi7 ___   Cmi7 ___   A♭mi7 ___   E♭mi7 ___

TWO-IN-ONE CHORDS
2a and 2b: Minor 6th/half-diminished 7th (minor 7 b5)

(2a) THE MINOR 6TH CHORD

To find a Minor 6th chord, simply lower the 3rd degree of a Major 6th chord. The chord is therefore a Minor chord with an added Major 6th interval from the Root Note.

It can function as either a leading chord or, in Jazz and Popular songs, as a final chord in a minor key.

WAYS TO WORK OUT A MINOR 6TH CHORD

(1) From the **Major Scale:** Build a sixth chord on the 2nd degree.

(2) From the **Harmonic Minor:** Build a sixth chord on the ivth degree.

(3) From the **Melodic Minor:** Build a sixth chord on either the 1st or 2nd degree. (Ascending Form).

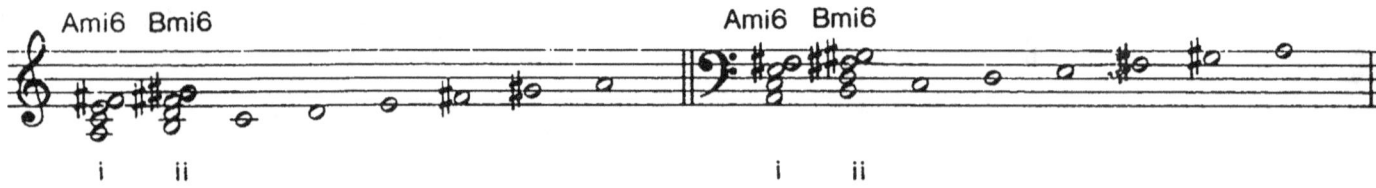

(4) From the **Modes:** Build a sixth chord on the 1st degree of the Dorian Mode.

(5) Using **3rds and 2nds:** Build up from the Root Note using a minor 3rd, a Major 3rd and a Major 2nd.

Minor 6th Chords (cont'd.)

(6) Using **Intervals:** From the Root Note use a Minor 3rd, a Perfect 5th and a Major 6th.

(7) From the **minor chord:** Add a Major 6th interval to the Minor triad.

(8) From the **Half-diminished 7th** (see next page) use the 1st inversion.

The chord symbol for a Minor Sixth chord is 'mi6'.

---

(1) Complete the following Minor 6th chords in Root Position.

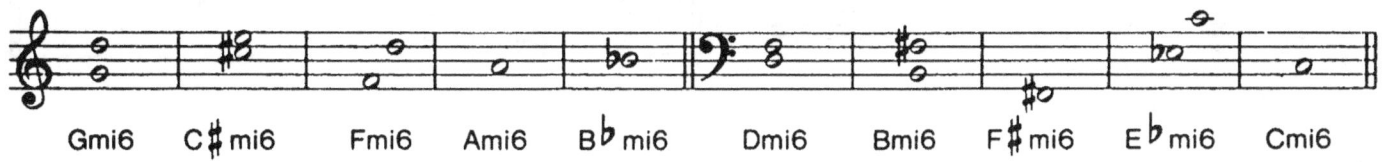

Gmi6   C♯mi6   Fmi6   Ami6   B♭mi6   Dmi6   Bmi6   F♯mi6   E♭mi6   Cmi6

(2) Write these Minor 6th chords in all inversions. Mark the Major 2nds thus: ⌐

A♭mi6   Emi6   Cmi6   F♯mi6

R   1st   2nd   3rd   R   1st   2nd   3rd   R   1st   2nd   3rd   R   1st   2nd   3rd

(3) Name these chords and mark the inversions.

NAME: _____ _____ _____ _____ _____ _____ _____ _____ _____

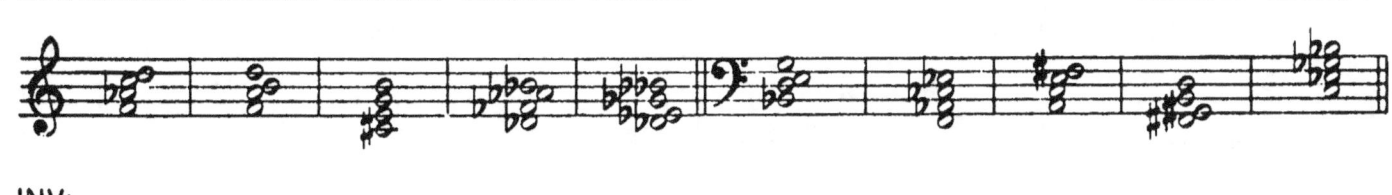

INV: _____ _____ _____ _____ _____ _____ _____ _____ _____

(2b) THE HALF-DIMINISHED 7TH OR MINOR 7TH FLATTENED 5TH CHORD

When the Minor 6th chord is inverted for the 3rd time (3rd inversion) it in fact becomes the Minor 7b5 or Half-Diminished 7th chord. The two names are used interchangeably. Some people prefer to work out the chord from the point of view of a Minor 7th chord, all that needs to be done is to flatten the fifth degree; other people prefer to see the chord as being similar to the Diminished 7th chord, the only difference being that the last interval (from the root note) is a minor 7th interval, not a diminished 7th interval. Hence the name Half-Diminished 7th, i.e. not quite a diminished 7th chord.

It is a 'leading function' chord and contains the Tritone. It is the extension of the diminished triad on the viith degree in a Major Scale.

WAYS TO WORK OUT THE HALF DIMINISHED 7TH OR MINOR 7TH FLAT 5 CHORD

(1) From the **Major scale:** Build a seventh chord on the viith degree.

(2) From the **Harmonic Minor scale:** Build a seventh chord on the iind degree.

(3) From the **Melodic Minor scale:** Build a seventh chord on the vith degree. (Ascending Form.)

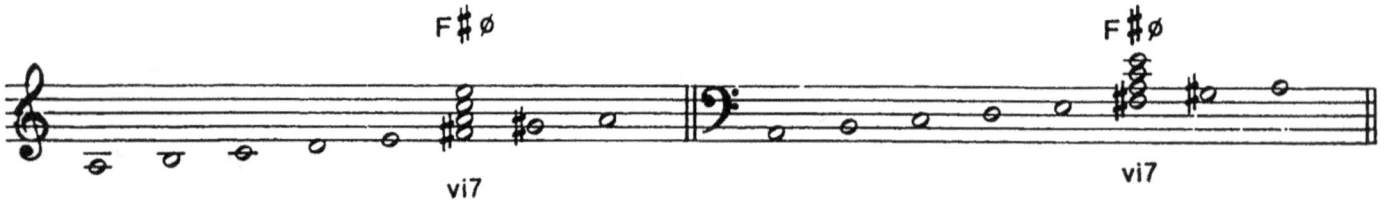

(4) From a **Mode:** Build a 7th chord on the 1st degree of the Locrian Mode.

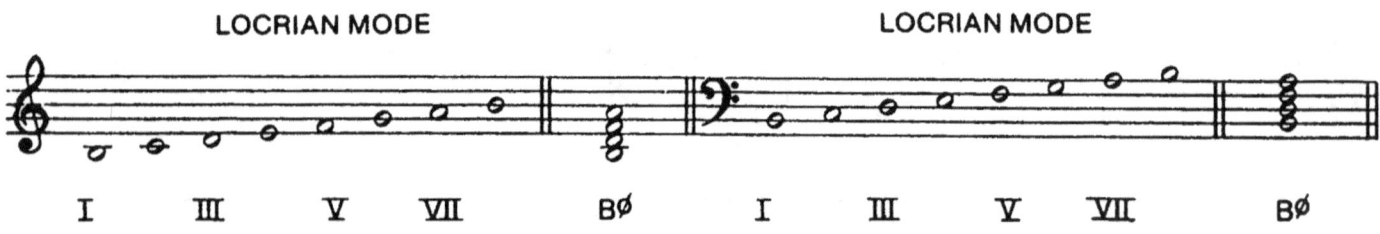

HALF-DIMINISHED 7THS (Mi7b5) (Cont'd.)

(5) Using **3rds**: Build up from the Root Note using a Minor 3rd, a Minor 3rd and a Major 3rd.

(6) Using **Intervals:** From the Root Note use a Minor 3rd, a Diminished 5th and a Minor 7th interval.

(7) From the **Diminished Triad:** Add a Minor 7th interval from the Root note to the diminished triad.

(8) From a **Minor 7th Chord:** Flatten the fifth degree.

(9) From a **Minor 6th chord:** Use the 3rd inversion of the chord.

The symbol for this chord is either 'mi7b5' or the diminished circle with a line through it, thus 'ø'.

---

(1) Complete the following Half-Diminished 7th chords (mi7b5) in Root Position.

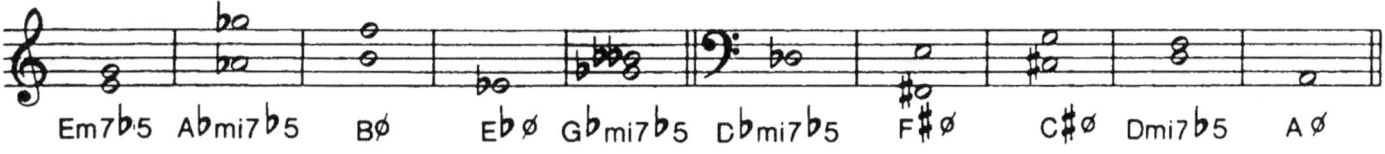

(2) Write the following Chords in all inversions.

(3) Write these Minor 6th chords and their equivalent Half-diminished 7ths in Root Position.

e.g.

Emi6 = C#ø   Gmi6 _____   A♭mi6 _____   Dmi6 _____

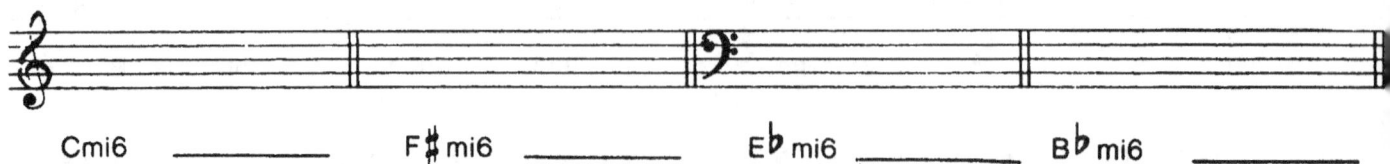

Cmi6 _____   F#mi6 _____   E♭mi6 _____   B♭mi6 _____

(4) Write these half-dim 7ths and their equivalent Minor 6ths in Root Pos.

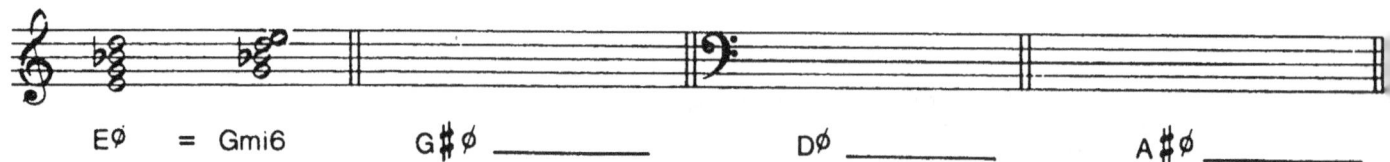

Eø = Gmi6   G#ø _____   Dø _____   A#ø _____

Bø _____   F#ø _____   F♭ø _____   Cø _____

(5) Name these chords and mark the inversions.

NAME: _____ _____ _____ _____ _____ _____ _____ _____ _____

INVERSION: _____ _____ _____ _____ _____ _____ _____ _____ _____

NAME: _____ _____ _____ _____ _____ _____ _____ _____ _____

INVERSION: _____ _____ _____ _____ _____ _____ _____ _____ _____

Fill in the chords below each of the melody notes in this song.

Do not harmonise those notes marked ∗.

Add a left hand accompaniment in the style shown on page 28.
In 4/4 time play a Bass note on the 1st and 3rd beats of the bar and play chords on the 2nd and 4th beats of the bar.

ALTERNATE CHORD SYMBOLS

The chord symbols used in this book are the recommended symbols in common usage. However they are not the **only** symbols in use in current publications.

The following are some of the alternate chord symbols found in hand-written charts and various publications.

Type of Chord	Recommended Symbol	Alternatives
Major Triad	C	Cma. Cmaj. Cmj.
Minor Triad	Cmi	Cm. Cmin. C−.
Augmented Triad	C+	Caug.
Diminished Triad	C°	Cdim.
Suspended 4th Triad	Csus4 or Csus	—
Major 6th	C6	C6th, C (add A). C(A).
Minor 6th	Cmi6	Cmin6. C−6.
Dominant 7th	C7	C7th. C (add Bb). C(Bb).
Major 7th	Cmaj7	CMA7. CM7. C.△
Minor 7th	Cmi7	Cm7. C−7.
Half-Diminished 7th	Cø or Cmi 7b5	—
Diminished 7th	Cdim7	C° C°7. Cd7.

In the following section on Altered chords, Flat and Sharp signs have been used to indicate the alterations. This is the manner recommended in this series.

In other publications, however, the alterations may be indicated by the use of Plus and Minus signs.

For Example: +5 indicates a sharpened or raised fifth.
 - 5 indicates a flattened or lowered fifth.

TWO-IN-ONE CHORDS
(3) DOMINANT 7TH FLATTENED 5TH

This chord is also the first of the ALTERED 7TH CHORDS. The chords previously learned in this book are the **basic** triads and 7ths. These basic chords have to be known as part of the basic vocabulary of chords, as there are no clues to the construction of the chord in the chord name or the chord symbol.

In the following ALTERED CHORDS, the instructions in the chord name are quite clear, providing you are familiar with the original chord.

DOMINANT 7TH FLATTENED 5TH

To find this chord simply follow the instructions. Take a Dominant 7th chord and Flatten the Fifth.

There are only '6' of these chord shapes owing to the fact that each chord becomes another 'Dom 7b5' when it is placed in the 2nd Inversion.

The chord has a strong leading function and is therefore used in the same way as the ordinary 'Dominant 7th chord'. Also, as it can be regarded as 2 chords in one, it can function as a Dominant Chord in TWO keys. For example, in its position as 'C7b5' the chord involved would lead to the Tonic Chord 'F'. The same chord in its position as 'Gb7b5' would lead to the Key of 'Cb'.

For this reason, this type of chord is often used as a 'substitute' chord.

WAYS TO WORK OUT A DOMINANT 7TH FLATTENED 5TH CHORD

(1) From the **Dominant 7th chord:** — Flatten the fifth.

(2) Using **Intervals:** From the Root Note use a Maj 3, Dim 5 and Min 7.

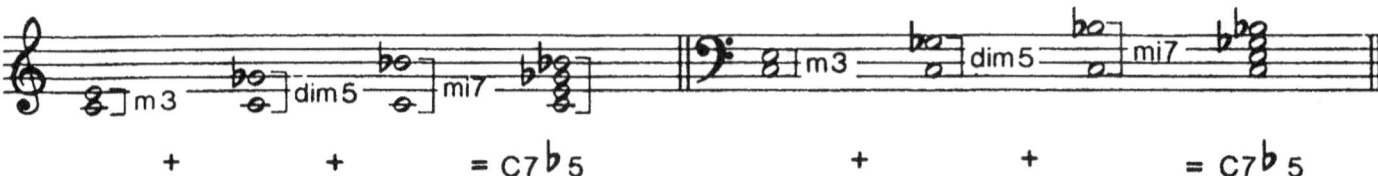

The chord symbol for a Dominant 7th chord with a Flattened Fifth is '7b5'.

(1) Write these chords in Root Position.

F7   F7♭5   B7   B7♭5   E♭7   E♭7♭5   A7   A7♭5   D♭7   D♭7♭5   G7   G7♭5

(2) Write the inversions of these Dom 7 b5 chords and mark the alternate names of the 2nd inversions of the chords.

e.g. D7♭5 —A♭7♭5   B♭7♭5 ____   F♯7♭5 ____   C7♭5 ____

R   1st   2nd   3rd   Root   1st   2nd   3rd   Root   1st   2nd   3rd   Root   1st   2nd   3rd

D♭7♭5 ____   A7♭5 ____   B7♭5 ____   E7♭5 ____

R   1st   2nd   3rd   Root   1st   2nd   3rd   Root   1st   2nd   3rd   Root   1st   2nd   3rd

(3) Name these Dominant 7th b5 chords and mark the inversions.

NAME: ____ ____ ____ ____ ____ ____ ____ ____ ____

INV: ____ ____ ____ ____ ____ ____ ____ ____ ____

(4) Resolve these Dominant 7thb5 chords in two ways.

e.g. C7♭5 = G♭7♭5   D7♭5 =   B♭7♭5 =   C♯7♭5 =

C7♭5 F   G♭7♭5 C♭ ____ ____ ____ ____ ____ ____

G7♭5 =   F7♭5 =   F♯7♭5 =   A7♭5 =

56 ALTERED CHORDS

(2) DOMINANT 7th SHARPENED FIFTH

This chord incorporates the Augmented triad and is frequently used because of this quality of sound. It also has a strong leading function.

The chord symbol for a Dominant 7th chord with a Sharpened Fifth is either '7♯5' or '7+'.

WAYS TO WORK OUT A DOMINANT 7TH SHARPENED FIFTH CHORD

(1) From the **Dominant 7th chord:** Sharpen the Fifth.

(2) Using **Intervals:** From the Root note use a Maj 3, an Aug 5 and a Min 7.

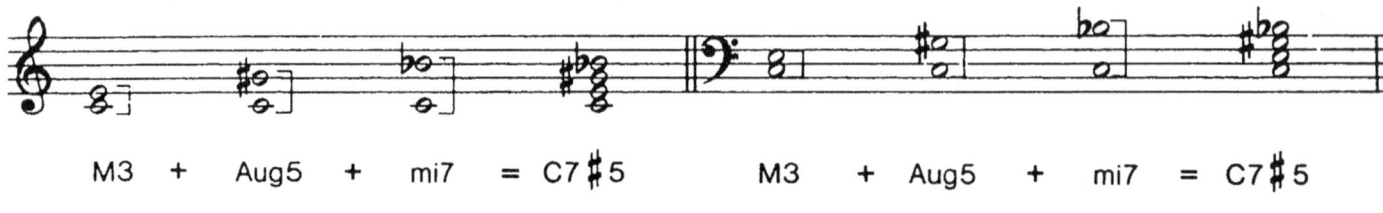

M3 + Aug5 + mi7 = C7♯5   M3 + Aug5 + mi7 = C7♯5

---

(1) Write these chords in Root position.
e.g.

F7 F7♯5 A♭7 A♭7♯5 E7 E7♯5 C♯7 C♯7♯5 D7 D7♯5 G7 G7♯5 D♭7 D♭7♯5 B7 B7♯5 F♯7 F♯7♯5 C7 C7♯5

(2) Write all the inversions of these Dom 7♯5 chords.

B♭7♯5   A7♯5   E♭7♯5   G7♯5

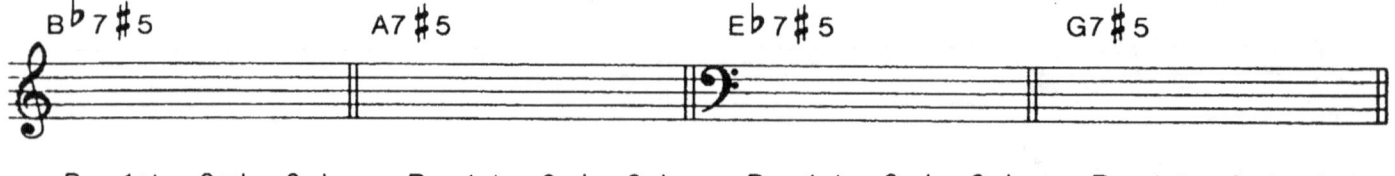

R 1st 2nd 3rd   R 1st 2nd 3rd   R 1st 2nd 3rd   R 1st 2nd 3rd

(3) Name these chords and mark the inversions.

NAME: _____ _____ _____ _____ _____ _____ _____ _____

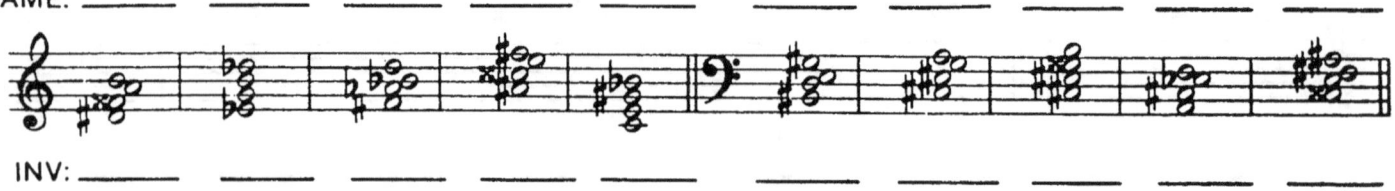

INV: _____ _____ _____ _____ _____ _____ _____ _____

ALTERED CHORDS 57

(3) MAJOR 7TH SHARP 5

This chord is found on the Mediant (III) of the Harmonic Minor scale. (See page 3). The sound of this seventh chord is half-way between a leading chord and a rest chord. Although it is generally used as a leading chord, it is also used as a final chord in some Jazz oriented pieces. Also look for this chord in Contemporary Classical compositions, where the composers are exploring the more unusual harmonies.

WAYS TO WORK OUT A MAJOR 7TH SHARPENED 5TH CHORD

(1) From the **Major 7th chord:** Sharpen the Fifth.

(2) Using **Intervals:** From the Root Note, use a Maj 3, Aug 5 and Maj 7.

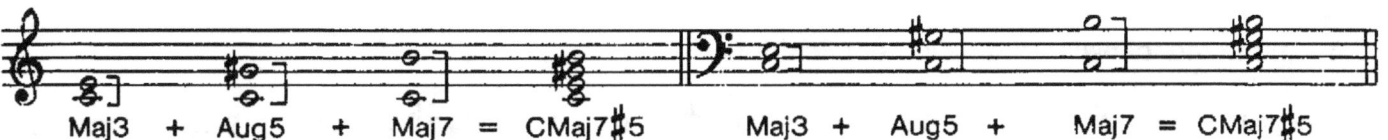

The chord symbol for a Major 7th chord with a Sharpened Fifth degree is 'Maj 7♯5'.

(4) MAJOR 7TH FLAT 5

As with the previous altered chord, (Maj 7♯5) this is also one of the more unusual chords. The chord shape itself (when written enharmonically) is often found as the top end of the Dominant 9(13) chord. (See Volume 2.)

The sound of the chord is dominated by the TRITONE, and the Flattened Fifth degree tends to make the chord sound very much like the Dominant Seventh chord of the Key a 5th higher. For example, the C Major 7th Flattened Fifth chord uses the notes C, E, G♭ and B. The G♭ is enharmonically the same as F♯. Comparing the notes of the D7 chord. to the C Maj7♭5, you will find that the TRITONE notes are the same. (C-F♯).

WAYS TO WORK OUT A MAJOR 7TH FLATTENED FIFTH CHORD

(1) From the **Major 7th chord:** Flatten the Fifth.

(2) Using **Intervals:** From the Root Note, use a Maj3, a Dim 5, and a Maj 7.

The chord symbol for a Major 7th chord with a Flattened Fifth degree is 'Maj 7 b5'.

58 Exercises.

(1) Write the following chords in Root Position.

EMaj7   EMaj7#5   A♭Maj7#5   BMaj7   BMaj7#5   E♭Maj7#5   CMaj7   CMaj7#5   B♭Maj7#5   F#Maj7

(2) Write the following Maj 7#5 chords in all inversions.

FMaj7#5   DMaj7#5   GMaj7#5   D♭Maj7#5

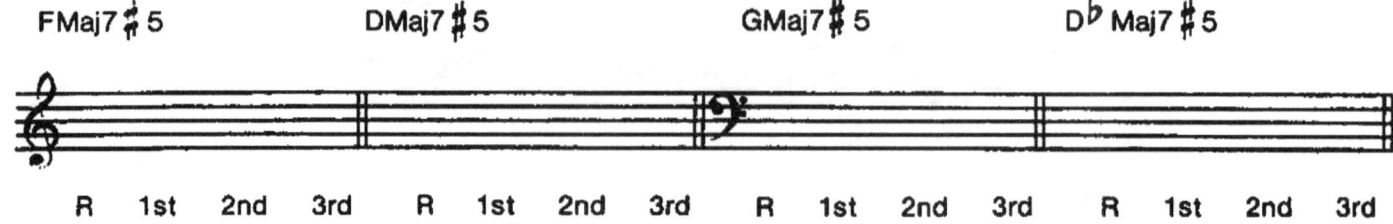

R 1st 2nd 3rd   R 1st 2nd 3rd   R 1st 2nd 3rd   R 1st 2nd 3rd

(3) Write the following chords in Root Position.

FMaj7   FMaj7♭5   A♭Maj7♭5   D♭Maj7♭5   EMaj7♭5   GMaj7   GMaj7♭5   CMaj7♭5   BMaj7♭5   C#Maj7♭5

(4) Write the following Maj 7♭5 chords in all inversions.

DMaj7♭5   F#Maj7♭5   AMaj7♭5   B♭Maj7♭5

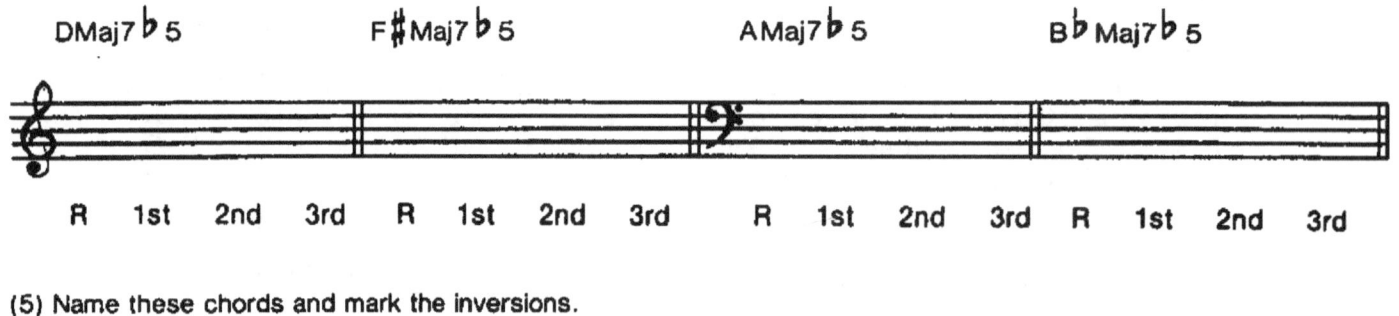

R 1st 2nd 3rd   R 1st 2nd 3rd   R 1st 2nd 3rd   R 1st 2nd 3rd

(5) Name these chords and mark the inversions.

NAME: _____ _____ _____ _____ _____ _____ _____ _____ _____ _____

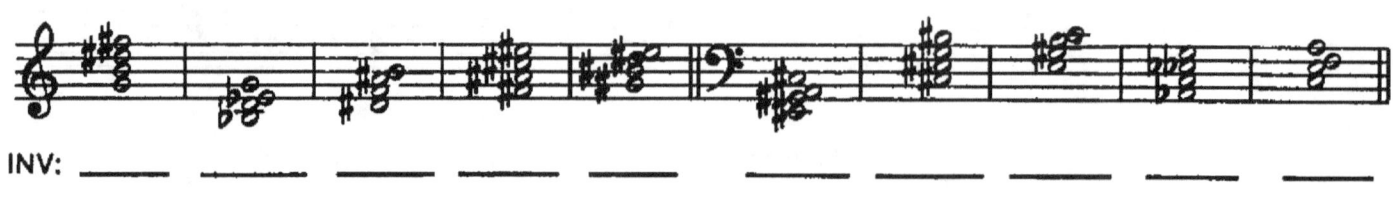

INV: _____ _____ _____ _____ _____ _____ _____ _____ _____ _____

NAME: _____ _____ _____ _____ _____ _____ _____ _____ _____ _____

INV: _____ _____ _____ _____ _____ _____ _____ _____ _____ _____

ALTERED CHORDS

(5) MINOR TRIAD WITH A SHARPENED 7th

The Minor Triad can be used with a Major 7th interval added to it, rather than the more usual minor 7th interval. The symbol used is 'mi♯7'. This chord can be found as the Tonic 7th chord in the Harmonic Minor scale. As such, this chord can be used as a final chord in a minor piece of music. It is also often used in a progression in which a melodic line moves in falling semitones over a constant triad. For instance, Dmi (D top note), Dmi♯7, Dmi7, Dmi6.

WAYS TO WORK OUT A MINOR ♯7 CHORD

(1) From the **Harmonic Minor scale:** Build a seventh chord on the Tonic Note of the scale.

(2) From a **Minor Triad:** Add a Major 7th interval from the Root note, to the triad.

(3) From a **Minor 7th chord:** Raise the seventh degree by a semitone.

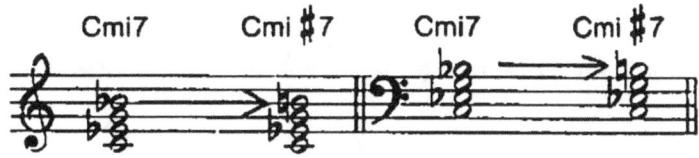

(4) Using **intervals:** From the Root Note, use a Min 3, Perf 5 and a Maj 7.

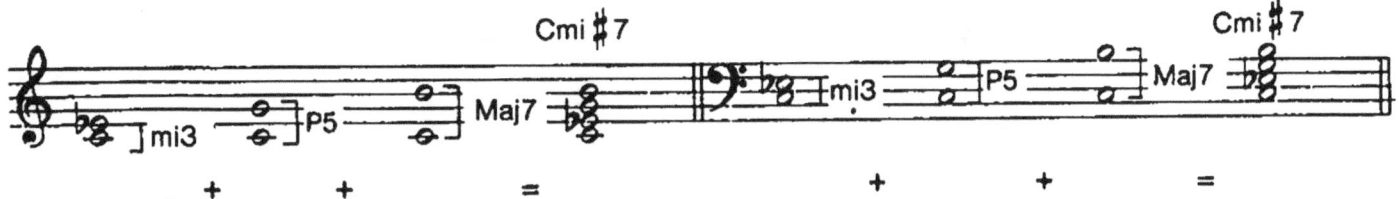

The chord symbol for a Minor Triad with an added Major 7th is 'mi♯7' or 'min(maj7)'

DOMINANT 7TH SUSPENDED 4TH CHORDS

This chord is an extension of the Suspended 4th triad. Once again the 3rd degree of the chord is replaced by the 4th degree of the scale.

There is a strong downward pull, from the 4th degree back to the 3rd degree, which is usually resolved in the following chord. (Mostly a Dom7 or sometimes a mi7 chord).

WAYS TO WORK OUT A DOMINANT 7TH SUSPENDED 4TH CHORD

(1) From a **Sus 4 Triad:** add an interval of a Minor 7th from the Root note, to the triad.

(2) From a **Dom 7th chord:** Replace the 3rd degree with the 4th degree.

(3) Using **Intervals:** From the Root Note, use a Perf 4, a Perf 5 and a Min 7.

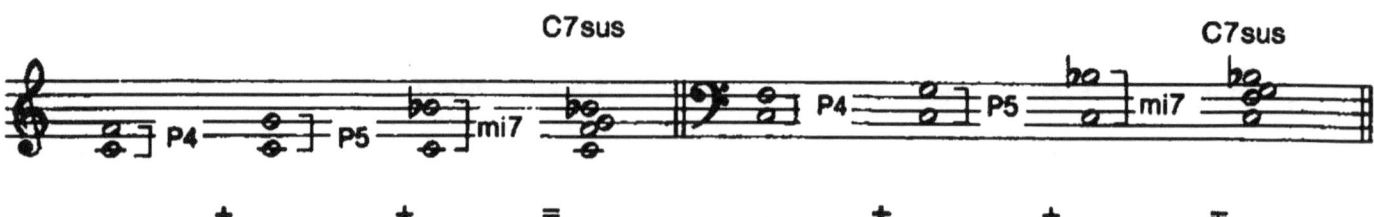

The chord symbol for a Dominant Seventh Chord with a suspended 4th is either '7 sus 4' or simply '7 sus', the 4 being understood.

(1) Complete these chords in Root Position.

(2) Write the following mi♯7 chords in all inversions.

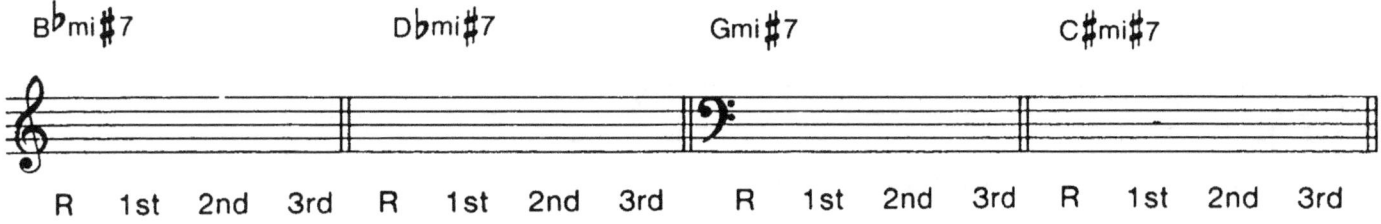

R   1st   2nd   3rd   R   1st   2nd   3rd   R   1st   2nd   3rd   R   1st   2nd   3rd

(3) Complete these Dom 7 sus 4 chords in Root Position.

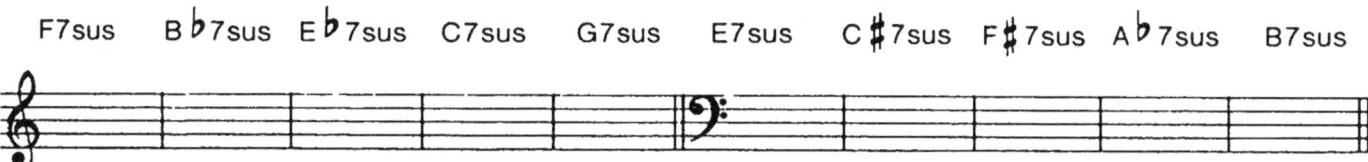

(4) Write the following chords in all inversions.

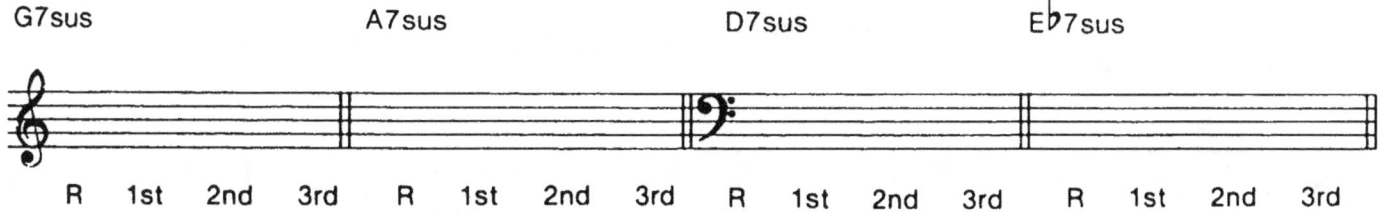

R   1st   2nd   3rd   R   1st   2nd   3rd   R   1st   2nd   3rd   R   1st   2nd   3rd

(5) Alter the following chords to match the chord symbols.

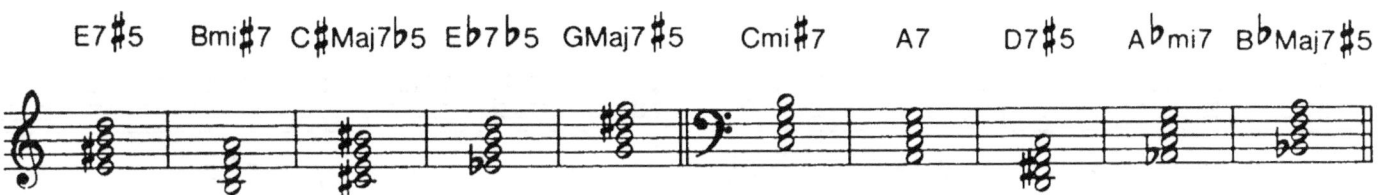

(6) Name these chords and mark the inversions.

NAME: _____ _____ _____ _____ _____ _____ _____ _____ _____ _____

INV: _____ _____ _____ _____ _____ _____ _____ _____ _____ _____

CHORD REVIEW EXERCISES

(1) Write these four-note chords in Root Position **above** the given notes.

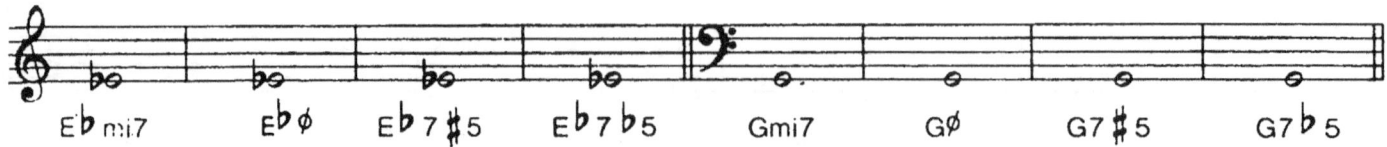

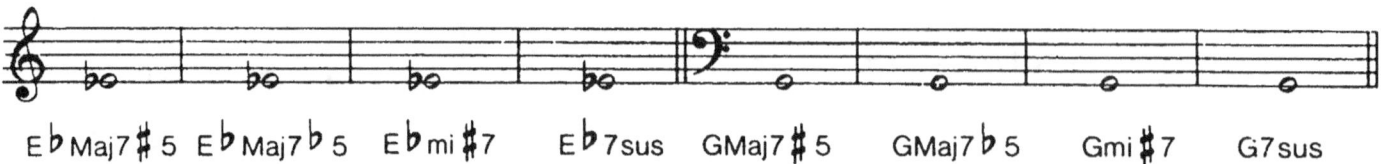

(2) Complete these four-note chords in Root Position, **below** the given notes and supply the chord names.

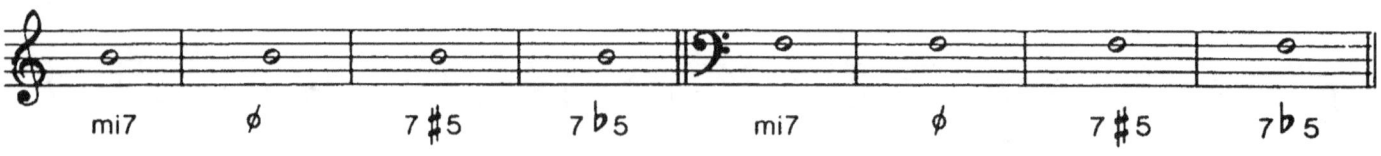

(3) Write and play the following chord progressions, based on the Cycle of Fifths. Make the 'voice-leading' smooth, by placing each chord in the nearest inversion to the previous chord.

Harmonise this melody by completing a four-note chord in the appropriate inversion, **below** each of the given notes.

In a tune such as this, where there are as many as four chord changes in one bar, it is better to play a single note bass line as a Left Hand accompaniment than to provide a Bass and Chord in the styles used for the previous two tunes in this book.

MOVIN' THE CHORDS AROUND

M.S. BRANDMAN